Walking
on my
Hands

Out of India – The Teenage Years

Jamila Gavin

First published in Great Britain in 2007
by Hodder Children's Books

Text copyright © Jamila Gavin 2007

The right of Jamila Gavin to be identified as the Author of this
Work has been asserted by her in accordance with the Copyright,
Designs and Patents Act 1988.

Back cover and chapter headings: © copyright Fred Chance
Picture 1: © copyright Museum of London
Picture 3: © copyright Graham Gower, from the
London Borough of Lambeth archives department
Picture 4: © copyright Corbis
Picture 13: © copyright Corbis
Picture 14: © copyright Michael Ward
All other photographs are from Jamila Gavin's
personal collection.

1

A Catalogue record for this book is available from the British Library

ISBN-10: 0 340 89449 0
ISBN-13: 978 0 340 89449 1

Typeset in Sabon by Avon DataSet Ltd,
Bidford on Avon, Warwickshire

Printed in the Uk by CPI Bookmarque, Croydon, CR0 4TD

The paper and board used in this paperback by Hodder Children's
Books are natural recyclable products made from wood grown in
sustainable forests. The manufacturing processes conform to the
environmental regulations of the country of origin.

Hodder Children's Books
a division of Hachette Children's Books
338 Euston Road
London NW1 3BH

Contents

In fond memory of Lucy

Chapter 1

Upside Down

'Why don't we start at the end and go all the way to the beginning again?'

(Alice's Adventures in Wonderland)

I was known as a daydreamer. I didn't concentrate enough at school. In my head, I was always walking on my hands. I walked on my hands till I was over sixty! Now I stand on my head – I can still do that. Perhaps it shakes my brains about. I think I did many things upside down and back to front – so it's taken me all my life to get things the right way round. One thing though, which I loved doing, upside down or the right way up, was listen to music, or sing and chant rhymes. So being a daydreamer didn't matter to me – as much as it did to my school teachers.

But then, my life hadn't ever been one straight line on a graph. It went up and down like a yo-yo! The same applied to my school reports, which read more like English weather reports: poor, fine, improving, could do better. The 'poor' bits usually applied to my Maths. I didn't start out bad at Arithmetic – I mean, I could do my sums: add, subtract, divide and rattle off my times tables; so I'm not sure when it all went wrong. Perhaps it was my haphazard schooling, veering between English primary and junior schools in London and Staffordshire and my schools in India: St Mary's Church of England School in Poona (or Pune as it is now called), and Woodstock, the American run school in the hill-station, Mussoorie, up in the mountains where I was born. Perhaps it was this which muddled me up, sent me into a numerical tizz from which I never recovered, so that by the time I was rising thirteen, at my highly academic girls' school in Ealing, London, I was seen as a puzzle: intelligent but stupid.

Why couldn't I read and write Hindi, if I'd lived in India for so long?

Yes, it was a puzzle – but they didn't bother to find out why, and I never thought to wonder why myself until long after: that English was my first language, that I went to an English school in India, that at home we only ever spoke English, that I only picked up Hindi with the street children and was only just beginning to learn it at school when we left; that I spoke, as so many Indians do, smatterings of Marathi, Punjabi and Urdu, and that my father, who spoke immaculate Urdu and should have passed it on to us, didn't, thinking it would only be a distraction. Later, I learned to speak passable French and German when I went on to study in Paris and Berlin – so I wasn't totally incapable.

Why couldn't I do Maths? Judgements were made without the right questions being asked, or a solution searched for. It was an age when to do badly had only one cause: laziness, and only one solution: punishment. So I had quite a tally of detentions and order marks throughout my later school life.

Music and English were my saving graces – especially music, though even my gift for music was queried by my school, as it was thought that people who were good at music should be equally good at Maths. It was one of those truisms which held sway and undermined me further. And although I loved drama, poetry, reading, and writing my own poems and stories, my grammar was sloppy and my spelling embarrassing – so I was not considered anything more than average at English, yet I had been reading since the age of three.

I always felt I should have been far more appreciated for my gymnastics. I fantasised about running away to join a circus. I could leap the horse as well as any; I could turn somersaults, perform cartwheels, shin up the ropes, hang from the bars, and – best of all – to the enormous admiration of my fellows, I could walk on my hands. I once walked the length of the gym hall! But I never got the much coveted gym medal, perhaps because, I argued to myself, they couldn't comprehend a girl who loved music, couldn't do Maths, and could walk on her hands. But it still rankles.

I know that this was the time that I began to feel that lump of depression which sat inside me and was to become a dark companion for many years. Then, every morning when I woke up, it was to a heavy, choking sensation which I could neither understand nor articulate. It was so deep inside that no one perceived it – for I was still a sociable person; still mischievous, adventurous and fond of jokes and laughing with my friends. I linked it to school – and so now, whenever I hear a child say, 'I hate school,' I remember my feelings, and wonder whether he is feeling the same as I had done – and I sympathise.

But my walk to school somehow dispersed my depression. I loved the smell of the early morning, the stammering blackbirds, trilling finches and scuttering squirrels, especially if it was sunny. I loved the sunbeams trickling through the leaves like runny honey so, by the time I arrived at the school gates, I was ready to take on the challenges of the day with energy and fun.

I do know – and always knew – that without my mother's absolute confidence in me, I would have gone under; been expelled or left school with nothing. Somehow, she never fretted; never nagged me about my homework; helped me when she could, often spoke up for me, and appreciated me, without being one of those ambitious mothers with Great Expectations for her child. I believe she herself was a genuinely good teacher – and appreciated what childhood was about. Later, I was to have difficulties with her about quite different things – but during my school days, she was my main strength and support.

I loved sleep almost more than being awake, for it was in sleep and in my dreams that I had adventures – adventures which felt far more real than anything I could imagine while I was awake. I dreamed of flying above the world, swimming in deep oceans, diving down into underground caves, where the sun's rays could barely penetrate. I dreamed of being carried along in the currents of swift rivers, and hurtling over waterfalls. I experienced extremes of emotion: ecstasy when I felt I was being absorbed into the sparkle of dancing light and the energy of water, and near-death terror when I swam among the heaving waves — glistening, shining, dark, fierce, mountainous waves, which could thrust me upwards to their peaks or overwhelm me completely.

Chapter 2

Crossing the Line

It was the coronation year of 1953, and the second of June found me walking the deserted silent streets of my west London neighbourhood.

I was seething with frustration. I shouldn't be here. I should be in central London, in the pitch of the crowds and excitement, with my cardboard periscope wobbling above the millions of craning heads. I was missing one of the greatest spectacles of my lifetime. I wanted to be there, hearing the reverberations of marching feet, horses' hooves and clattering carriages; the bellowed commands, the patient, merry crowds singing and joking; the sudden bursts of music from the different military bands positioned along the way, the snare drums thundering across the Mall and St James's Gardens, down the winding canyons of streets running between those high imposing buildings of the city, all festooned with the red, white and blue of fluttering flags, posies of flowers and decorations, and excited spectators leaning perilously out of the window, piled one on top of the other. I would have braved the struggle in the heaving streets, buffeted among the waves of crowds, which surged, rose and fell in their desperate attempts to see the military parades and the carriage processions, while people challenged each other to identify the dignitaries and representatives from every country in the world, such as colonial rulers like the Sultan of Zanzibar and the Queen of Tonga.

Oh the Queen of Tonga,
Came to Britain from faraway,
Oh the Queen of Tonga,
Came to Britain for Coro-na-tion Day
sang the calypso.

The carriage processions trundle by, bearing the heads of state, presidents and prime ministers; there goes Prime Minister Robert Menzies of Australia, Jawaharlal Nehru of India, Khwaja Nazimuddin of Pakistan, and Mr St Laurent of Canada. A rolling ecstatic cheer sends the pigeons and starlings whirling into the air, creating their own formations, as the nation's hero and prime minister, the Right Honourable Winston Churchill rides by. Here come the carriages of the princes and princesses of the Blood Royal, and the crowds heave with extra surges of excitement as the glass coach is spotted, carrying the Queen Mother and Princess Margaret. But most of all, everyone is trying to defy the laws of gravity in their attempts to see the great golden carriage, drawn by eight grey horses, carrying Queen Elizabeth, with Philip, Duke of Edinburgh, sitting alongside her, to Westminster Abbey to be crowned Queen Elizabeth II.

But I wasn't there. I wasn't even in front of a television set. I was walking the streets of an alien

London suburb – an area of Ealing where we had never lived before – which felt as foreign and unconnected to me as if it had been a corner of Timbuctoo.

We had deserted my father and brother in India, in the interests – as my mother always insisted – of making sure I had a chance to pursue my music, as suggested to her by a visiting Trinity College of Music examiner who had stayed with us in Poona. He had noticed that I loved composing, and that I had a particular affinity with the minor key.

So earlier that year, my mother and I, and my young five-year-old sister, Romie, had left India, embarking on an Italian ocean liner which had docked at Bombay, on its way from Sydney, Australia, to Southampton in England. We were leaving my father behind in his new job in Bombay, and my brother in his boarding school in Poona. My mother, strong-minded, a mixture of rash impetuosity and absolute certainty, had decided that only in England could I, in particular, get the right education and music teaching she thought I needed. I was still that rather free-spirited child, playing the piano, composing, writing, acting and dancing – but like a butterfly, not for exams and achievement, not for my mother's ambition, let alone mine, but just for the sheer pleasure; sucking life as a bee sucks the juice of flowers.

Where the bee sucks, there suck I
In a cowslip's bell I lie,

as Shakespeare wrote, and I used to sing, with my mother at the piano, accompanying me in the song by the eighteenth-century composer, Thomas Arne.

Among the British passengers, the ship had been packed with excited patriotic Australians on their way to London for the coronation. The mood on board was full of jollity. This was to be the start of the new Elizabethan Age.

Some people were leaving Australia for the first time, and determined to experience everything. Traditionally, in those days of sea voyages, there was a ceremony for 'Crossing the Line' – crossing the equator! Even though, by the time the ship reached Bombay from Sydney, it had already crossed the line, the ceremony was saved for those of us joining the ship later. It took place on deck, bordering the swimming pool. Someone dressed up as Neptune, with a wig of flowing hair, embedded with shells and sea objects. He sat on a makeshift throne with trident in hand, surrounded by young women in mermaid costumes, combing their hair with giant combs. It was all like a great pantomime, culminating with people being thrown into the swimming pool – clothes and all! Oh the laughter, the fun, and the friendship – I'm glad I didn't realise this would be my last voyage on an ocean liner.

This was the voyage when I spent almost every waking hour in the swimming pool. I loved the sea and water so much that I not only swore I'd marry a sea captain, but would also have my ashes scattered at sea when I died.

I was up each morning at dawn to watch the crew fill up the deep hold, which acted as a swimming pool. I loved climbing the steel ladder down, down, down to the bottom, then, as the water level rose, bobbing up and up with it. If I was the first in the pool each dawn, I was often the last person in the pool at night before they emptied it, floating around and looking at the bright stars in a black sky.

Crossing the Line seems symbolic now. We were crossing our own line into a new life – a life in England. Because my father had already become an absent father, I hardly thought about him; didn't understand for years how distraught he had been when we left, and how helpless he had felt against my mother's fierce determination. Yet maybe, in a deep way, his trauma and her guilt entered my subconscious, and became a part of the inexplicable unhappiness I was to feel for so long.

But all that excited anticipation of arriving in England for the coronation blotted everything out. This was a new England. A nation which had been through the Second World War, and the gloom and distress of destruction, loss and bereavement was now in a state of frenzied excitement, determined to see in the second Elizabethan Age.

Some people recall the Fifties as being dreary and grey, but for many it was like spring breaking out after a grey and desperate winter, when everyone wanted to forget the hardship and deprivation of those war years. Colour came back. The excitement of the coronation meant suddenly everyone was painting their houses in bright glossy colours and, in a spirit of fervent patriotism, gardens which had been turned over to vegetables gave way to flowers again – especially red, white and blue flowers. Fashion became flamboyant. In came wide, flowery skirts with heaps of lace petticoats, natty boleros and dotty little hats; in came the Teddy boys, with their slicked-back hair, tight Edwardian-style suits and pointy winkle-picker shoes. Black-and-white film was swept away by technicolor, and music, which had ached with nostalgia, gave way to skiffle, swing and rock and roll.

There was feverish building all over London. As part of the new age, they had constructed a new concert hall on the desolation of the South Bank. The Royal Festival Hall was built to replace the Queen's Hall, which had been bombed. It was a modern building constructed with modern materials; concrete, glass and wood; controversial but dynamic – though perhaps because audiences had suffered the extreme echo of the other great musical venue, the Royal Albert Hall, they produced in the Royal Festival Hall an acoustic which was so dry that, years later, the conductor, Simon Rattle, was to complain that it took out of him the will to live.

A programme of slum and bomb site clearance was underway. There was a mood to be modern and to rethink how people should live; how to create homes which wouldn't turn into slums. There were still acres of prefabs – simple temporary homes knocked up quickly to house people made homeless by the war.

Down in the jungle living in a tent,
Better than a prefab; no rent,
we used to chant.

What, though, could ever be better than the

palace we had once lived in, in the Punjab? This palace of many rooms, terraces and verandahs; the palace in which we had lived during the first five years of my life, which dominated my imagination, and which my father had transformed into a College of Further Education.

But I looked at the prefabs with curiosity. Like the bungalows we also lived in, in India, they had no upstairs. I found them quaint and almost like toy houses. And as for the bomb sites, they were dangerous but exciting playgrounds, with their shattered walls, exposed rooms, and weed-filled foundations.

However, on that Coronation Day, I too was infected with the excitement, and couldn't bear the fact that I wasn't in the centre of London. My sister was only five years old, and no doubt my mother felt she couldn't cope with two children in those teeming and excitable crowds.

On that day, we three were alone in our new house. We hadn't yet got to know our neighbours or make friends. Of course, the radio was on, and my mother was glued to the live broadcast – listening to the sounds and vivid, heart-stirring music: '*Zadok the priest and Nathan the prophet anoint-ed Sol-o-mon King!*' rang out from behind the net curtains. And then the shouts of 'Vivat! Vivat! Vivat! Regina is the Queen, Vivat!' which can still make the hairs stand up on the back of my neck.

Descriptions of the event by the BBC commentators only made me more desperate to be up in central London and, finally, I fled our little house to wander alone, wishful, fretful and feeling deprived. I would be twelve years old that August – on the cusp of adolescence – my childhood slipping away.

Every evening at dusk, they closed the great iron gates to the park. But somehow, in my dream, I was inside the gates, with the whole park to myself. The playground gleamed empty in the moonlight. The swings shifted with a gentle metallic clink of chains in a soft night breeze; no children clung to the iron steps leading up to the

18

high metal slide, waiting their turn to swoop down to the concrete ground below. The umbrella swing, the roundabout and the fearsome, death-defying American swing, were all motionless – yet as if waiting. And then I saw them; merged into the shadows of each piece of equipment, was a fairy – just like the flower fairies, except these were playground fairies. With the park to themselves, and the human children all safely in bed, they crept out with glee, and leaped upon the swings and roundabouts. I was there. I hadn't grown up yet. I saw them.

Chapter 3

The Sins of
the Mother

Because we had moved around so much, travelled so much, nowhere had ever seemed a permanent state of being. We were never anywhere 'for ever', and this rootlessness seemed an essential part of the whole adventure of our lives with our journeys between India and England. I seemed to live inside and outside with the same kind of freedom I had had in India – but on that Coronation Day, I sensed we were going to be here for a very long time. Maybe for ever – whatever that may mean.

My mother had not been happy for a long time.

It had started in Batala, in the Punjab, with the death of her third child, my baby brother Sushil John. I knew then that something profound had changed. I became aware of unhappiness. For years after, I put everything untoward down to that event, although I didn't know of the conflict that had surrounded his death until my parents were in their old age.

My mother had been convinced that Sushil must be born in an English-run hospital, while my father preferred her to go to a nearer one, albeit run by Indian doctors and nurses. As usual, her stubborn persistence prevailed, and she went to the English-run hospital in Amritsar. But her trust in the English doctor was misplaced. Did she expect to be treated like an English patient? Or because of her marriage to an Indian, was she discriminated against? The hygiene was pitiful. She described how the sweepers (the women who cleaned the bathrooms and lavatories) trailed their brooms through the ward, leaving germs in their wake. Perhaps it was sheer negligence and nothing to

21

do with who she was, but her newborn boy, Sushil, developed an infection and within three weeks was dead.

It was 1946, and our life in Batala was soon to end. Indian independence had been agreed; Jawaharlal Nehru was to be its first Prime Minister, and Mahatma Gandhi, who had brought to the world the concept of *Satyaghara*, 'Peaceful Resistance', continued as its spiritual leader. But the large Muslim minority led by Mohammed Ali Jinnah wanted their own homeland. The mayhem which followed, and the murderous conflict between Hindus and Muslims, was to result in the last act by the departing British rulers: the division of India – a partition. The terrible events during Partition, which was to split India into two, creating Pakistan, split my family too. It sent my mother fleeing to England with her two children, leaving my father in Batala. Batala was in the Punjab, on the very line which was to divide India and Pakistan, but it was an area which the Sikhs considered to be their homeland. My father bravely stayed to oversee his beloved college being turned into a refugee camp, as each day he risked death from the bands of Hindus, Muslims and Sikhs, all trying to assert their boundaries and separate religious identities.

When it was all over, millions were dead. India was independent, Pakistan was born, and the British began to leave. This was the beginning of the end of Empire.

The Church Missionary Society, who had funded and supported my father's dream of transforming the palace into a college, decided to pull out. Baring Christian College, as it was now known, was to continue under another Christian body, and this new group wanted to put in their own people. It was a truly bitter blow.

So in 1949 my father was sent by the CMS to be principal of St Mary's Teacher Training College far, far away from the Punjab, in Poona (now called Pune), near Bombay. When the news of my father's appointment reached us in England my mother was delirious with happiness. I remember her almost skipping down the road, my hand in hers, as she sang, 'Poona, Poona, Poona – where the colonels come from!' (Poona had been a well-known British army base.) 'We're going to Poona.' It was one of the few moments since Sushil's death that I can remember her being so unreservedly happy and optimistic. The war was over, Partition was over, Batala and the palace had gone, yes – and Gandhi had been shockingly assassinated – but my father had a good job, and we were going back to India to join him, and he would see his new daughter, Romie, already nearly two years old.

If my mother was happy, I was happy – though I wondered how it would affect my ambitions to become a child film star! Those were the days of child stars like Shirley Temple, Margaret O'Brien and Elizabeth Taylor. Those were the days when the British film industry was at its peak – right there in Ealing, in the studios next door to the library we used. We often went to the cinema, and I was familiar with the faces of those stars of Ealing films: Alec Guinness, John Mills, Jean Simmons and Margaret Lockwood – and of course the Hollywood stars, such as Stewart Granger, Cary Grant, Ava Gardner and Betty Grable.

When I knew we were returning to India, I insisted on going to the entrance of Ealing Studios. I approached the most important man I could see – he was wearing a uniform with shiny silver buttons. I told him that I wanted to be a child star, but that unfortunately, I was about to go back to India. Would he kindly let me know if a part came up for me, I asked. He agreed to take down my name and address, and promised to let me know.

The call never came – and it was years before I realised that I had approached the commissionaire.

However, my mother's happiness in Poona was short-lived. She was restless, perhaps lonely. She was an intellectual, with a greedy mind which craved the stimulus of ideas and debate. In Poona she was isolated. It must have already dawned on her that her marriage to my father – I believe entered into with innocence and joy and love –

had thrown her into a social limbo. She had committed a racial 'sin', broken a taboo: a white woman marrying a brown-skinned man, an Indian; and, even worse, she had produced three half-caste children – undeniable evidence of her crime. Because she was so strong, and never admitted to depression, sadness or any negative feelings, I wasn't aware that my white mother had violated one of the deepest social taboos of her time. She was powerfully protective of her children, instilling in us the conviction that we were as good as anybody. I believe that she must have been repeating the same words of encouragement which her father may have said to her when she was growing up.

If belief in the racial superiority of white Anglo-Saxons over all others was one central tenet of those times, so was class. The world in which my mother grew up was one in which everyone knew their class, their station and its duties. 'Class' was a word one heard constantly, along with 'snobbery' and 'breeding'. Another widely heard word was 'common'. To be called 'common' was one of the most scathing insults you could receive. The way you spoke: your accent, education, background and family status, defined you completely. To be described as having 'breeding' was a compliment.

My mother's family was located at various positions along the entire spectrum of what could be labelled 'middle class' – with parts of it ranging from lower middle class to upper middle class. Some would probably have been described by the extraordinary term 'sunken middle class' – meaning someone who had either married beneath them, or gone down in the world. My mother's mother came from the Woods family, respected Staffordshire potters, associated with the Whealdons and Wedgwoods. My grandfather Dean opted out of his profession as an artist and potter and, in what seemed like an act of defiance, transformed himself into a shopkeeper. Was this move from artisan to shopkeeper a march up the social scale, or a fall in the wrong direction – into 'sunken middle class'? Perhaps he simply wanted to be his own boss, but it put him somewhere down the lower ranks of middle class, though other parts of the family were at the other, higher end of the spectrum: some were farmers, others were in business, and wealthy. They sent their daughters to Roedean, drove limousines and lived in country houses.

Perhaps my grandfather saw in my mother the means of his own redemption. Perhaps it was frustrated intellectual ambition that turned him into a difficult and unsociable man. Like him, my mother was highly intelligent. She personified everything he would have wanted for himself. He had nurtured in her an interest in philosophy, literature and music; he taught her to play the piano, so well that she could ramble through Beethoven sonatas, Schubert's *Moments Musicaux* and Mendelssohn's *Songs Without Words*. Her brains got her a scholarship to Ornie Girls, a well-known Staffordshire school, and then offers of scholarships to both Oxford and Cambridge, choosing Cambridge – something my grandfather never had the opportunity to do.

He knew that she would be mixing with people who were mainly from social backgrounds higher than hers. He would have known and understood all the problems my mother was having to deal with and, just as he himself had faced them head on, so did she. Grandfather Dean had instilled in her the same advice which she later instilled in us: 'You are as good as anybody – just remember that. Don't let anybody put you down.'

But what did he say when she decided to marry an Indian? I asked this question when my mother was alive, but never got an answer from her. After all, she didn't elope. She didn't present him with a *fait accompli* but had gone through the formalities of an engagement. This wasn't a shotgun wedding. She left Persia, where they had met, both of them teaching with the Church Missionary Society, and had come home to announce to her parents that she was marrying an Indian: she would be going to live in India – thousands of miles away, a journey taking three or more weeks by sea, with only the possibility of very occasional visits home. They would have had every opportunity to dissuade her. I asked her what on earth they had thought, but she always brushed aside my question.

After my mother died, I asked an older cousin who could remember the event. She said. 'Grandma and Grandpa were devastated. They felt they had sacrificed everything for her.' They had tried to stop her. Her father refused to see her off when she finally left on her long journey from Staffordshire to Victoria Station in London, to catch the boat train to Southampton, and then board a ship for the three-week sea voyage to Bombay. She had been accompanied as far as Victoria by her mother and eldest brother. Harold. My cousin told me that my mother had cried all the way to London – so bitterly that Harold had said, 'You don't have to go, you know. You can just turn round right now.' But she was adamant, and through her tears had cried, 'I don't want to change my mind.'

Had she any idea what prejudice she would face?

'Racial prejudice' didn't mean quite the same

thing then as it does today. Britain had not experienced the large-scale immigration from Africa and the Indian subcontinent as happened later. What was commonly believed in was racial superiority; racial purity. They used words like 'good stock' and 'breeding', as though people were horses or dogs. If you mixed breeds (or races) then, like animals, you were inferior – you were a mongrel – less valuable. But this was of course ignorance, as so-called 'British people', as much as any other people on the globe, have constantly moved, inter-married, and mixed their blood, their genes and their cultures.

I now realise that, living at that time, my mother would have experienced a good deal of ostracism from the vast majority of the British, whether in India or in England. Thinking back, I can't remember any English friends in India. Perhaps that's why I recall the word 'missionary' expressed with disgust, as even from them she experienced massive rejection. Perhaps this led to my utter scepticism of religious people. Ah me! But I was to learn also, that nearly all races have this same abhorrence of mixed races – not least the Hindus; they too, not accepting that they themselves are a product of racial mixing from time immemorial. The subcontinent was known as 'the melting pot'. After all, the Aryan people who composed the religious works called the Vedas (like the Bible of the Hindus) were pastoralists, who were supposed to have come into India from Central Asia over five thousand years ago. Other Aryan tribes went North into Europe, forming what became known as the Germanic people.

Adolf Hitler encouraged Indians to think of themselves as fellow Aryans – especially in his attempt to make them rebel against the British. In 1939 India was pushing fiercely for independence from Britain. Indian contingents formed a large part of the British army fighting against Hitler, but some Indian politicians and freedom fighters like Chandra Bose asked, 'Why should we fight our enemy's enemy?' and even went to Germany to talk to Hitler. But others in India were swayed by the powerful philosophical message of

Mahatma Gandhi, who favoured *Satyaghara* – Peaceful Resistance – and who, unlike Hitler, believed in a secular, multicultural society. My family was bound to be Gandhian.

The Indians were as colour-conscious as any European – perhaps more so – aware of every nuance from light to dark, the matrimonial columns in their newspapers reflecting the search for 'wheat-coloured' girls. At that time in South Africa, a black person couldn't sit on the same bench as a white person. In India, lower castes couldn't draw water from the same well as upper castes, and an untouchable couldn't even walk in the shade of a Brahmin.

The Poona we were living in now was a little different. It was post-Independence, and within the schools there were Indians, British and Anglo-Indians – but probably still no one with whom my mother could form deep friendships. So just as her father had invested himself in her, she now invested herself in me; she had taught me to read and write, taught me my first few words in

French, taught me the poems of Walter de la Mare and Christina Rossetti, Robert Louis Stevenson and Shakespeare. She passed on to me her intense love of Beethoven, Schubert and Mendelssohn, and her love of the piano. One year when were going up into the cool of the hills for the summer, we called in at a music shop in Dehra Dun, before taking the winding road up to Mussoorie. We asked for any records of classical music. They only had one work, an orchestral piece by Saint-Saëns, who I had never heard of. From reading the label, I gathered that it was called *Omphale's Spinning Wheel*. I used to call it 'Omfail's Spinning Wheel'! We took it anyway and I played it incessantly – winding up the gramophone and setting the steel needle onto the rotating record. The orchestral sounds resonated down the hillside and reached the ears of a missionary living in a bungalow lower down the hill.

'What music's that?' she asked.

'Omfail's Spinning Wheel,' I replied. (It was years before I realised Saint-Saëns was a French composer, and his piece was called in French, *Le*

Rouet d'Omphale.) I knew she liked it, because from then on she allowed me to sit on the swinging lounger on her verandah. But that was the extent of any contact with us.

In my dream, my brother and I played on the steep slopes of Landour above Mussoorie, slithering helplessly on the pine needles. My mother had always instilled in us a rule – never run down a hill unless you know where the bottom is. This was the foothills of the Himalayas, where streams and cataracts hurtled down the gullies, where paths wound round the mountains like thin threads, where precipices fell a thousand feet. But my brother and I were chasing each other thoughtlessly, and suddenly my feet lost their grip on the pine needles. I was hurtling down the slope out of control, trying desperately to catch on to something, and then I went over the edge of a precipice – one which dropped down for ever into oblivion. I was falling, falling, falling, and far above, I could hear my brother's voice calling out, 'Jamila's dead, Jamila's dead!'

* * *

In 1951, my father had decided to leave education
and take up a prime job with the newly formed
Government of India Tourist Department. It
meant him moving to Bombay, but my mother
had refused to go, arguing that the intense humid
heat of Bombay wouldn't suit her health. Poona
was higher in the Deccan hills, with a cooler and
drier climate. So now we were in Poona and he in
Bombay, and the tensions increased. My father
had robust health and was never ill. Though my
mother too was generally healthy, she felt he
never understood the condition she had suffered
from, particularly in the heat, when her legs
would swell and she would develop a fever. In the
family, we got used to her having 'an attack' and
would say, 'Mother's got a leg!' – which meant
that a rash had appeared, signalling the onset of
an attack. So from an early age, I had got used to
coping with her 'leg'. She could put no pressure
on it all, and would have to take to her bed for a
few days, and we got used to fetching and
carrying.

At my mother's deathbed in 1997, I was moved when my sister gently lifted aside the sheet and touched her feet – we both knew how, ever since my mother was a young girl of sixteen, she had struggled with all the embarrassment and inconvenience of this condition, and that it had dominated her life in a disproportionate way. Now, it was all over.

Had my mother experienced the same melancholy I felt? Her generation were brought up to keep 'a stiff upper lip', to 'lie on the bed they had made'. The word 'depression' was not a part of her vocabulary. In those days you just 'got on with it'. And yet perhaps she transmitted some of her innate sadness to me – which got deeper inside me as I got older, and was no better now that we were living in England.

Chapter 4

A House of Our Own

Previously, whenever we had come to England from India, we had always stayed in one of the large, crumbling houses off Ealing Broadway; three-storey houses which had once been grand, with large bay windows, flights of stone steps leading up to imposing doors with porticos and balustrades, with basement gardens in the front and huge gardens at the back with trees. Never mind that now, post-war, a whole lifestyle had vanished and they had been turned into flats, become neglected, the gardens overgrown – some so much so, that they were as impenetrable as the forest of thorns which had grown round the palace in which Sleeping Beauty lay. No matter that the bare hallways and stairs were freezing in winter, that the bathrooms had long, deep white baths above which hung terrifying gas-fired water-heaters which had a reputation for blowing up, or that one risked freezing to death sitting on the dark lavatories at the end of a gloomy hallway. Never mind that, when we lived in those flats, we had to feed their spluttering gas fires with endless piles of pennies and sixpences, and that I never had my own room – it was all a part of my imaginative landscape. I was the Little Princess of Frances Hodgson Burnett, I was Cinderella, or Cloak O' Rushes, I was the Little Mermaid. I could identify with Oliver in *Oliver Twist*, or Pip in *Great Expectations*. I could endure poverty and hardship so long as there was something to strive for; so long as it was part of an unfolding adventure.

My territory had never been confined to the bricks and mortar of home. It extended beyond the boundaries of garden wall or fence – like a bird or a fox, I had my domains and haunts; in India, they had been the guava and mango groves around the palace, the towering sugar cane fields, the paths through wheat fields lurking with snakes, the ruined Muslim mausoleums, the water tank jumping with frogs, the muddy banks of the lake which had been part of a palace garden. And then there was the excitement of the bazaars, with their hanging saris, glittering jewellery, carpets and cloth; the delineation of bazaars into their different craft components: ironworkers, stone masons, carpenters and leather-workers, with the rhythmic sounds of hammering, chiselling, sawing and carving like some extraordinary percussion section of an orchestra.

In England, there was both the real territory of streets, alleyways, bomb sites and churches, and an imaginary geography of invented zones where demons lurked, spies spied and strange creatures roamed the night. I climbed trees – all the way up to the top, as if I were a scout observing the lie of the land. This was in Walpole Park, where children and dogs ran free: avenues of mature trees, winding walks, the huge pond with mysterious islands in the middle where the water birds made their nests and where royal swans ruled supreme, arching their wings with a terrifying display of might if they perceived an enemy such as an innocently threatening child, or a dog.

The green spaces flowing away among flower beds became transformed into the canyons and winding tracks of the Wild West. I played cowboys and Indians; Indians stalked cowboys, and cowboys galloped around on horses, and I galloped too on my imaginary horse, across the park behind the library. How I galloped under low-hanging bushes as if crouched over the neck of my horse, wheeling and jumping and, sometimes, flinging myself to the ground, or ducking behind bushes to have fierce gunfights with outlaws or prowling Indians.

But the only horses I ever got near to for a long time were the cobs which pulled the milk carts, the shire horses which pulled the brewery coaches: great towering beasts, with their *clip-clopping* hooves; or the much smaller horse who trotted around with the rag-and-bone man. The man would call out, 'Rag bone! Rag bone!' I understood the rag, but wondered about the bone. What bone? Whose bones? He was the equivalent of today's recycling bins, taking away anything from old saucepans to unwanted sofas.

I went ice skating at Richmond ice rink, where a live orchestra played Strauss waltzes, Spanish tangos and *Masquerade* by Katchachurian. Whenever I hear that music, I can feel the chill of the ice, the wind the skaters made as they swished past, with the women's skirts flipping this way and that as they spun, revealing the twist of their bodies, the line of their thighs, the strength of their legs, and I can hear the sound of steel blades cutting their edges into the ice. I had ballet lessons, and danced through fantasies of tutus and pink silken ballet shoes. I was Violetta Elvin or Tamara Karsavina, I was Margot Fonteyn, Beryl Gray or Moira Shearer. But I was also me . . . 'I can do that!' I was sure I could do anything if only I practised.

But most of all, there was my music; I sang and played the piano constantly, composing songs and pieces. (But to my school teachers, I was lazy.) We may have been poor, living sometimes in only two rooms, but we were never without a piano. It was always tucked into some corner, along with the cooker and the kitchen sink – and I can still smile when going into houses now, larger than I could have ever imagined, which have no piano, and the owners say sadly, 'We've simply nowhere to put it!'

To have a house of her own had been my mother's strongest desire throughout my life. We had always lived in houses which belonged to my father's job – even the palace we had lived in in the Punjab had not been owned by us, and now it was a College of Further Education – a fulfilment of my father's vision. In India, we had resided in bungalows belonging to the schools where my parents taught. In England, we lived in rented bedsits. So I knew, in my limited child's way, how thrilled my mother would be to fulfil her ambition and walk through her own front door.

But what kind of house would it be? In my mind, our new house would be burrowed beneath the roots of a tree, as in *Peter Pan*; or it was a mansion full of rooms and stairways, of towers and garrets, as in *Sleeping Beauty*; it was entered through mysterious gardens and gateways, as in Frances Hodgson Burnett's *Secret Garden*; or a little country cottage, as in *Little Grey Rabbit*. It could even be a house created under a table, full of dark mystery extending far beyond the four table legs.

After a gruelling school week teaching Latin and Religious Studies, my mother's greatest pleasure was in setting forth at weekends, with sheaves of property details, to look around houses for sale. They were always roomy, rural houses set into leafy gardens; they had bay windows facing south. 'I love south-facing windows!' she would exclaim – as though that was an imperative to anything she would think of buying – 'and they must be windows with a view.'

It was all a fantasy, of course – but I didn't know. I didn't know that you needed money – quite a lot of it – to be able to buy a house at all. What could she afford on a teacher's small salary? My father was unable to send money from India because of currency restrictions.

One day, soon after arriving in that coronation year, we left that half-imagined land off Ealing Broadway, with its alleyways and basement steps, its vast overgrown gardens, and busy commercialism, and moved to another part; a place as alien as if it had been on another planet. My mother had never taken us to look at houses like these on our house hunts. We had never looked at small terraced houses embedded in suburbia, in streets tightly packed with rows of two-storey terraced houses, and gardens the size of pocket handkerchiefs; for this is what my mother was showing us. This was where we were going to live. It froze my imagination and left me struck dumb.

The *For Sale* sign identified our new home: a small house, which was sealed into a terrace of others, all looking the same, without one

centimetre between them. Rose bushes impri-
soned into crazy paving looked as desperate as I
felt. My spirit was numbed, my fantasies killed
stone dead. I wasn't being rational or fair, and it
was certainly not a feeling I could express or
explain at the time. If it had south-facing
windows, it was irrelevant; whatever views there
were, were just of the same houses opposite. My
silent disappointment must have spoken volumes.
'Look!' cried my mother consolingly. 'We have a
park on our doorstep.' It was true. Just over the
road was a park, which was to be the main saving
grace – though it never had the excitement of
Walpole Park, it was to become an essential part
of our territory.

I accepted this new home. I had to. But I still
dream of houses – and sometimes wonder
whether the houses in my dreams exist
somewhere, and that maybe I appear in them as a
ghost, wandering from room to room.

*I dreamed I was in a vast mansion of many
rooms. I wandered up staircases and along*

corridors, and came to a room whose door was partly ajar. I peered inside to see a red-haired boy crouched in the middle of a four-poster bed, surrounded by tall pillars of books. His arms and legs were long and thin and angular, and he reminded me of a spider devouring its prey as he reached for one book after another, read it at a glance and tossed it aside. He read with such intensity that the characters leaped out from the pages of the books, alive – and, some of them, very threatening.

A woman appeared at my side. I knew she was his mother, and I said with alarm, 'Should he be reading quite so many books? It seems bad for him.'

She shrugged despairingly.

Chapter 5

She Shall Have Music

Every Saturday during term time meant a ride on the Underground – alone – all the way to the West End, to Trinity College of Music, where I was a Junior Exhibitioner. I never minded going – even though it meant missing Saturday morning pictures at the local cinema. I loved my piano and violin lessons, and my wonderful teachers: my piano teacher, Jean Jukes, who quietly guided me through those early years, and wasn't surprised when they talked of me becoming a performer, my violin teacher, Len Smith, who loved to joke; he had learned two Hindi words which he reversed with glee. 'Juldi kurro!' (hurry up) he would beam when I came into the room, and then laughingly cry, 'Kuldi jurro!' as I unpacked my violin. There was the choir, where we sang songs by Janáček, Brahms, Mozart, Fauré and Handel; and the musicianship class taken by the legendary Gladys Puttick, who always encouraged her children, and whose musicianship was awesome. She valued my talents – my playing, my ability to improvise and compose. She was to restore my self-esteem when, later, I crashed to my lowest ebb.

Round the corner in Mandeville Place was the Wallace Collection, with its wide-ranging array of paintings, statues of marble and bronze, Elizabethan miniatures by Nicholas Hilliard, and the amazing collection of suits of armour and weaponry from all round the world. Often I would go alone there to eat my sandwich lunch in the inner courtyard, and then wander round the galleries to look at the paintings. Just as I could recognise composers by their music – the difference between Bach and Mozart, Beethoven, or Brahms – so I wanted to educate my eye in the differences between the French painters, the English, Italian and the Dutch, all of which were handsomely represented at the Wallace Collection: Constable, Gainsborough, Poussin, Fragonard, Canaletto, Steen or Van Hooch. I didn't just educate my eye, I learned to love the pictures: the pretty Fragonard girl on the swing, flying high above the leafy bushes and branches of trees, being spied on by a young man; the icy Dutch canals of Jan Steen; and those interiors of homes by Van Hooch. I knew what Venice looked like long before I ever went there, from the paintings by Canaletto.

At the far end of Marleybone High Street was a little antiques and second-hand jewellery shop called Hildebrand. It was nearly opposite Dinely Studios, the music studios which Trinity used as an overspill. I was often going down that road and from the age of thirteen I had started wandering into this shop. I loved staring through the window at the display: the pieces of china, the figurines, the clocks, the bejewelled rings, brooches, bracelets and necklaces. One day I ventured in. The shop was run by a shortish, sandy-haired man with a kindly face, called Mr Hildebrand. He allowed me to browse.

Just as I had trained my eye to recognise different schools of painting in the Wallace Collection, so, with Mr Hildebrand's help, I began to learn the names of the huge variety of jewels and precious stones which fascinated me: sapphires, rubies, garnets, opals, emeralds, pearls, diamonds – and so many more. He told me he was in exile from South Africa because he disapproved of apartheid*, and we used to chat about all sorts of issues in the world. I sometimes witnessed odd transactions. Once a shabby man shuffled in off the street and, from an inside pocket of his raincoat, he produced a brown paper bag, from which he extricated a glorious necklace glinting with rubies and diamonds. He and Mr Hildebrand discussed it in detail, then the shabby man left, leaving behind the necklace.

*Separate Development: A system of racial segregation based on colour as enforced in South Africa by the white ruling minority government.

Mr Hildebrand put it round my neck and told me it was worth thousands of pounds.

I had my eye on a pair of china figures, and I wanted to buy them, but they were about fifteen pounds, and I couldn't possibly find that kind of money. In those days, fifteen pounds was a lot. It was to be the amount I earned per week when I later joined the BBC. He said, 'I'll put them aside for you, and you can pay me what you can, when you can.'

So I did. Each Saturday, between Musicianship class and choir, I went all the way down Marylebone Road to Mr Hildebrand with my tiny payments, often made up of pennies and sixpences from my pocket money until, at last, one day, I paid the whole thing off.

Many years later, having gone abroad and lost touch with Mr Hildebrand, the Great Train Robbery took place. I read in the paper that, earlier, an antiques shop on the Marylebone Road had been broken into and raided by the train robbers, who needed cash ahead of the train robbery to pay their cohorts. I read that the proprietor, Mr Hildebrand, had been wounded in a scuffle. I was astonished. Was that *my* Mr Hildebrand? Next time I passed by and went to his shop, it was closed down. It felt like another chapter in my life had closed.

Chapter 6

Aimez-vous Brahms?

I'll never forget the day I walked into my girls' high school for the first time. It was arranged so quickly, I wasn't even wearing the strict regulation uniform when, mid-term in June 1953, I entered those hallowed portals. Instead of the navy-blue gymslip, white shirt with the distinctive red-stitched edging on the collar and the navy velour hat, I wore grey. How embarrassing! How I stood out as the 'new girl', joining them late. But I would have stood out anyway, for I was the only brown-skinned child in a school of seven hundred pupils. Indeed, I was the only brown-skinned child in the whole of

Ealing, and our name, Singh, shortened from Khushal-Singh, was the only Indian name in the telephone book.

I remember everyone's head turning to look at me, their faces full of curiosity. Even as I stood in the doorway of the classroom, I was picking out girls who I felt would be my friends. There was Susanna, with her long, thick, reddish-brown plaits, who reminded me of Anne of Green Gables. Ann – without an 'e' – nicknamed Gibby, with her kind rosy face, and hair the colour of shiny autumn conkers. And Anne – with an 'e' – they called Kenwright, with her tight blonde curls and muscular legs, who always seemed to prance and toss her head, as if she wished that she were a horse.

I was welcomed among them and quickly made friends, and within the week was also kitted out in my regulation uniform.

It was an imposing school, the high front door approached by a flight of stone steps, opening into an oak-panelled lobby with wooden floors. An elegant wooden staircase with a shining banister (which many of us surreptitiously, on pain of dire and unusual punishments, slid down) led to the upper floors and the classrooms. At the base of the staircase was the headmistress's office, and outside her office was a large, shining wooden elephant complete with howdah, on which you were sent to sit if you had misbehaved in class. Once I found myself sitting there when the headmistress passed by. The look she cast me was one of great disappointment as she said, 'Not you, Jamila?'

But there were many areas of the school I loved: the large light gymnasium, with its bars all round the walls and great loops of ropes hanging from the ceiling; the music room, with its piano and percussion instruments; the solemn oak-panelled library, where you studied in complete silence; the lawns and tennis courts outside. Yet I remember early winter nights, when darkness fell before we had left school, when I stood on an upper floor, staring out of the windows across the lights twinkling round the neighbourhood, feeling a sense of deep desolation.

* * *

You need to live the best part of a lifetime to understand which people and events put you on the path which has taken you to where you are now. As much as I seemed to live in a state of deep despair at school, the despair was inner. Outwardly, I flitted about as gaily as a butterfly, plunging myself into all the activities I loved, while disregarding the subjects which I arrogantly thought were totally irrelevant to my life. I was failing at Maths – well, who needs Maths? I was blundering my way through Physics and Chemistry – what on earth could they do for me? And wasn't Latin a language *'as dead as dead can be, it killed the ancient Romans, and now it's killing me'*? What use were these subjects to me, when all I wanted to be was a musician? So long as I could sing in the choir, be in school plays, enter the poetry competitions, write poems and stories; so long as I could play the piano and compose, what on earth did anything else matter? The 'second string to your bow' philosophy was abhorrent to me – 'You must have a second string in case you fail, and will need to look for some other kind of job'. Me fail? To even entertain such a thought was a failure in itself. It was like standing at the brink of a chasm and thinking, *If I don't leap across, I won't get to the other side. If my leap isn't good enough, I'll fall into the chasm. Perhaps I should turn back.* No. There was no turning back. It was jump or die. That's how I felt at school.

Was I right or wrong? Probably a bit of both. I was wrong to believe that *any* knowledge was useless, however irrelevant it may have seemed at the time. But the good news is that knowledge is not just confined to school – it may have taken fifty years, but I have learned to be fascinated and thrilled by the physics and chemistry which makes up our bodies, our minds, our nature and life on earth, and our universe. I can still draw on my minuscule knowledge of Latin – to relish words, their origins, and their connections with so many other European languages. My parents, both good linguists, had made me conscious of the origins of language and culture – this word is

Arabic, or that has its roots in Sanskrit; this Latin, that Greek – and that so many words and terms embedded in the English language came from India and beyond. Within the British Isles it was fascinating to know that place names were Saxon, Viking, Roman or Norman – sometimes running into each other. It brought alive the sense that races and religions have been on the move, mixing and merging, since time began. I know now that, upside down or back to front, nothing is irrelevant.

In every school I had ever been to, each pupil had their own desk – wooden, with a flip-up lid. The inside of that lid reflected the pupil's passions and identity. Scratched onto the wood were the names of their heroes and heroines. Pinned up were pictures of adored film stars and pop stars, boyfriends and crushes, all surrounding the school timetable. The pop idol of my school was Cliff Richard – yes, 'that boy from Lucknow' as my father always added when he joined us later, knowing that Cliff Richard had been born in

India and came from the city of Lucknow, where we too had relatives.

So who was pinned up inside my desk lid?

Aimez-vous Brahms? (The title of a book by Françoise Sagan, which was to become famous later.) Do I love Brahms! He was my first passion; my discovery; I felt I owned him. No one commented, or sneered, or thought it odd, that my pin-up was a postcard portrait of the composer Brahms – an old man with a long beard! I had just discovered the music of Brahms, and had been swept away with as much excitement as if I'd discovered America. The first gramophone record I ever bought with my own money was of Brahms.

Another friend at school was Atarah Ben-Tovim, a superb flautist, who went on to become a top professional player. Atarah always seemed grown up – yet smiley and bubbling with enthusiasm. We had made headlines together at a school concert; she playing her flute, and me my own composition on the piano. The headline of the local paper said: *Two Talented Schoolgirls*. It made our school feel some pride in us.

Atarah was a Junior Exhibitioner at the Royal Academy of Music, while I was going to Trinity College of Music. But for both of us, music was the most important thing.

During the summer holidays, Atarah played with the London Schools Symphony Orchestra. I was so envious. I wished I played an orchestral instrument well enough to have joined an orchestra. Instead, I sometimes went along to watch them rehearsing in preparation for a concert.

That summer, she told me of a schoolboy pianist who was going to be playing a Mozart piano concerto with them and asked if perhaps I'd like to observe. Of course I would, I replied, and every day for a week I attended the rehearsals just to see this young pianist, wondering if that could ever be me. Probably not, I thought. I didn't really think I would ever be a concert pianist, and this boy already performing in public was younger than me. But it didn't matter. I just enjoyed watching him. It also meant sitting through the other orchestral works they were playing, works I didn't know, and didn't think I was paying attention to.

But one night I was in bed, drifting off to sleep, and heard from a distance an orchestral concert my mother was listening to on the radio. Suddenly I sat up. I knew the music they were playing. I jumped out of bed in a state of high excitement. I knew every note of it – but I didn't know why I knew it, or what it was.

I listened avidly through to the end.

'That was . . .' said the announcer, 'Brahms's Fourth Symphony . . .' It was the symphony that the London Schools Symphony Orchestra had been rehearsing during the week I had attended.

'I love Brahms!' I cried, and as soon as I could, I rushed off with hard-saved pocket money, and bought Brahms's Fourth Symphony. It was a Deutsche Grammophon recording, conducted by Eugene Jochum. I then went on to discover Brahms's other symphonies, his *Requiem*, all his piano music, his chamber music and, most adored of all, his violin concerto and piano concertos. Gradually, as I acquired them, I played them – the records, I mean – over and over, hovering above the large wooden radiogram we had in a corner of the room, ready to lift the arm and play my favourite sections again and again. I always knew I would never be able to play those piano concertos myself. They needed the strength of a man, though one or two women have played them, like Marta Argerich and Gina Bachauer. But I had no illusions. I was a thin, scraggy creature in those days, with very small hands. I would never play those concertos.

At school, the music teacher was enterprising and brave. Instead of training the choir in the more ladylike songs such as *Nymphs and Shepherds*, she got us singing Brahms's hot-blooded *Gypsy Songs*. How marvellous.

Roses bloom all in a row in summertime,
Lads will after lassies go, and that's no crime.
Gracious me! If kissing were a sin,
All this worldwide place long since
A waste had been.
Not to marry, that's the sin!

An older girl, Joyce Bailey, higher up the school, who was a very good pianist, played the *Second Rhapsody in G minor Op. 79* by Brahms at a school concert. She had come first in a local music festival – and it was she who was to become my first idol, on whom I modelled myself. Again, I rushed out and bought the music, and soon taught myself to play it, and its companion, the *First Rhapsody in B minor*. I was besotted, and soon acquired some of Brahms's *Intermezzi*, teaching myself to play them by listening to a recording of Walter Gieseking. From then on, for a while, all my piano compositions were like Brahms.

When Joyce Bailey left to follow a profession in music after her A Levels, I gave her as a leaving present the figurines I'd bought from Mr Hildebrand, because she had so inspired me with her Brahms, and for being such an example and icon for me.

But hey! I had become a teenager. Shouldn't I have been thinking about boys, fashion, film stars, pop music, independence, rebelling – not Brahms? This was the Fifties; the dawn of the age of teenage power, rock and roll, Bill Haley and the Comets – whose films were closing down cinemas because of teenage hysteria; the dawn of the age of 'The King' – Elvis Presley. I heard one of his songs one day – 'Blue Suede Shoes'. It was as strange as strange could be to my ears, yet compulsive and beguiling. I went home and told my mother breathlessly, 'I've just heard some Elvis Presley.'

'Have you really, dear!' she said – and I had no idea whether she had ever heard of him before either.

I look at some of the children's books we were reading in the Fifties: writers such as Philip Saville, Noel Streatfeild, and Jeffery Farnol; stories about school, horses, ballet dancers and historical tales. I read the so-called boys' books too: Tarzan, Biggles and Jennings. Then there were comics; American comics like *Superman* – which many parents objected to – and British ones like *Girl, Eagle,* and *School Friend* – which they didn't object to because they promoted upright values and standards. Girls and boys read about duty, loyalty, bravery and sacrifice. I was totally inspired by the women I read about in *Girl*: missionaries and reformers like Gladys Aylward, Mary Slessor, and Elizabeth Fry. Great achievers like Sonje Henje the ice skater, Margot Fonteyn the ballet dancer, and Mary Rand the athlete. I gobbled up detective fiction from Agatha Christie to Marjorie Allingham, Ngaio Marsh and Geoffrey Household. I was also reading George Eliot, Charlotte Brontë, and her sisters Anne and Emily. Edgar Allan Poe was another favourite, feeding my appetite for the macabre. All good stuff, but none of which reflected the world we were growing up in. There was nothing which dealt with the present-day world of becoming girlfriends, wives and wage-earners; with the nitty-gritty of adolescence or sex, or the new commercialism of the rapidly changing world we now lived in, ready to pounce on the recently acquired wealth which lined our pockets.

At school my friends and I didn't talk clothes or make-up, boys or sex. There may have been some barely whispered comments about a particular girl who had boasted about having a boyfriend, and possibly imparted mysterious details about their relationship, but we were like the children in those *Girl* comics – unworldly, by today's standards; kept in ignorance, or – as the adults would prefer to describe it – kept in a state of innocence.

Yet I wasn't innocent – and hadn't been for years. Children are often way ahead of their parents. There were always older girls to impart all kinds of information, and I had long ago glimpsed other kinds of comics too: comics for adults with love stories and illustrations of men kissing women, which I found stirring and extraordinary. Although my mother and I went to the cinema regularly, and there we saw stories and images all about men and women falling in love – perhaps creating an impossible ideal – the difference was that this was about romantic love; not marriage, not sex. Yes, we were mostly ignorant about sex. We knew the facts of life – that was taught us at school in Biology, and learned from our more worldly friends; but we didn't know how to deal with the dilemmas such as, when do you know that sex means love? Or that sex doesn't mean love? How could you make a boy stay with you and refuse him sex – when they so often insisted that you couldn't possibly love them if you didn't give in. And – most important of all – if you were going to break the cardinal rule of no sex before marriage, how did you stop yourself having a baby? The pill had not yet been invented, and contraception was not spoken of at all – at least, not by anyone I knew. I remember one girl coming to school in a panic because she had 'done it!' and now had a terrifying wait until her next period before knowing whether she was pregnant. To be unmarried and pregnant in those days was to be plunged into shame and ignominy, with the strong likelihood of your baby being handed over for adoption – though many sought out back-street abortions, a criminal offence until abortion was legalised.

At this time, there was full employment – in fact, more jobs than workers – which is why politicians began to encourage immigration from the old colonies. The steamship *Windrush* had arrived in 1948, filled with enthusiastic people from the Caribbean hoping that the streets of London would be paved with gold. There was no problem getting a job, but there was a problem getting accommodation in bomb-ruined London – and they soon discovered that the streets were not paved with gold, and that the enthusiasm of those from the Caribbean was not reciprocated by the locals! Just as the Irish and Jews and other immigrants in the past had suffered racism and discrimination, so did the new arrivals. Yet how swiftly their culture spread into the mainstream; by the time I was at my high school we were singing Jamaican songs:

> *Carry me ackee go a Linstead Market*
> *Not a quattie would sell . .*

They had raised the school-leaving age from fourteen to fifteen, and most boys and girls left to go into work, which meant they had money in their pockets. The new music from America cast aside those romantic, crooning balladeers like Frank Sinatra and Bing Crosby, and hurtled in – yes, like comets – rock bands and singers full of primitive, rhythmic, sexy energy. It was the age of the teenager.

People were terrified. I remember some cinemas refused to show wild, hip-gyrating films, and the BBC often censored the music, refusing to broadcast it because it might corrupt the nation's youth.

But I was hardly engaged with this seething world, which was changing the face of society. I was lost in my own world of music and my own composing. Up until then, my main musical influences had been Beethoven, Brahms and Schubert – and I had composed many songs which my school choir sang. I had set to music one of my favourite of Hans Andersen's fairytales, *The Red Shoes*, composing songs and descriptive music. This was to bring about one of the events which I look back on as a pivotal event in my life – though I didn't appreciate it at the time. It was all because of Lucy.

Chapter 7

Lucy

Lucy arrived at the school after me; another new girl. Ripples of excitement had run through the school. It was rumoured that Lucy was the daughter of the nationally famous forces sweetheart and television presenter Mary Malcolm. Television was still in its infancy. It was still live rather than recorded, it was still a novelty and viewed with huge interest and curiosity. It was the start of home-grown celebrity, and anyone who appeared on television was someone to be in awe of; touched with gold. Everyone was as excited as if it had been royalty coming to join us. I remember being less fascinated, because we

large rooms furnished with beautiful furniture, long flowing curtains, and amazing wallpapers of all kinds of colours and designs. I remembered that by going to her home I stepped into another world of film stars and actors: of personalities who were family friends, like the conductor Sir Malcolm Sargent and actress Rachel Kempson. Lucy's mother, who was stunningly beautiful, was the granddaughter of Lily Langtry, the famous Edwardian beauty and mistress of Edward, Prince of Wales. Her father was a playwright, Sir Basil Bartlett – a knight, a gentleman, a theatrical and a rogue, who was terribly handsome and charming. To eat at her house was to sit down to a meal in a grand dining room at a table large enough to seat six, or eight, or even more people; that we ate food I had never even known of before: food cooked the French or Italian way, vegetables unknown to me, salads with exotic dressings – and they ate spaghetti, which I had never experienced before! One of their friends, a film star called John Fraser, knew how to twiddle it round his fork, the

Italian way, and I practised and practised till I too could do it.

On the occasions that I was invited to her home, I was treated with such warmth and – just as importantly – with great appreciation. They loved me playing the piano. They listened to my compositions and encouraged me with enthusiasm. But my friendship with Lucy gave me contact to this other world: the world of the media, film, theatre and television. When they heard some of the music I had composed for *Red Shoes* they immediately thought I should go on a children's television programme called *All Your Own*.

At that time, another household name, Cliff Michelmore, was running *All Your Own*, and an appointment was made for me to see him. It was 1955. BBC Television Centre was still a building site, but one day I picked my way across the rubble to a temporary mobile office – and there he was. We talked about it – and his idea was that I should get my school to put on a production which he could then feature in the programme.

There are times when I can be ridiculously literal. If the programme was called *All Your Own*, then surely I must do everything myself? But I needed the help of the school – especially the music teacher. But oh dear! I was not at all skilled in diplomacy. Although I wanted her authority and experience to help me set up rehearsals, and make sure that my disparate friends turned up and learned their parts, I insisted on being in control of the music and directing the play. But everything went horribly wrong. She got fed up with me, and I with her, and then my main singer – such a good singer she was too – said she didn't want to do it, and the whole enterprise collapsed. I was distraught and helpless, with no idea how to achieve a production. It was a bitter moment. I knew it must be my fault. I knew that I should have handed over to my teacher. But I have a stubborn streak which, like all qualities, can be a strength as well as a weakness. In this case it was major weakness.

* * *

I was in a room in total darkness. I was in a panic. I must get out, I must get out. But I couldn't find the door. I groped all round the walls, desperately trying to find the way out, and then I fell to my hands and knees, and crawled across the floor, seeking a trapdoor, or anything that would let me out.

Somehow, all was not lost. Although I couldn't get a production off the ground, I was invited to appear on my own to sing and play from *Red Shoes*. This was still an age when all television was live; and it would be like any live performance on stage. First, I was to go to an address in Holland Park to meet Huw Weldon, who was the interviewer for *All Your Own* (later to become Controller of BBC Television) – and here was another example of my stubbornness. I insisted I was perfectly all right to attend the interview on my own, but once on the Tube realised that all I knew was that the meeting was in Holland Park – I had no address and no idea where it was.

In 1955, a brown-skinned girl like me was still rather rare – and I often attracted attention. I was particularly used to men who had been soldiers out in India approaching me to tell me of their experiences and how they had loved being there. But sometimes their approaches weren't innocent, and I was not very good at having strategies to get myself out of a pickle. As I sat on the Tube, on my way to Holland Park and this oh-so-important interview, a man started to talk to me. He began to shower me with compliments, telling me I was the most beautiful girl he had ever seen. I began to feel uncomfortable, especially when I got off at Holland Park and he did too. He followed me out into the street. What was I to do? I couldn't even look as though I knew where I was going, because I didn't. In my moment of utter helplessness, I heard a voice saying, 'That child's with me!' It was as if my guardian angel had miraculously appeared. I felt a hand on my arm as Joanna Simons, the producer of the programme, forthrightly steered me away. I was saved.

Sitting in the lobby when we arrived was a cluster of boys and girls, all of them with their mothers or guardians. Some were conjurers or painters, some were good with their hands; others had made marvellous constructions, or were singers and musicians of various kinds, like me.

My moment came to be interviewed by Huw Weldon. I was to show him what I was going to do; that I would play a *Nocturne* by Chopin, and then he would talk to me about *Red Shoes*, and I would sing and play some extracts.

When I entered the room, there was Huw Weldon sitting at a table and over to one side was a large grand piano. The only times I ever played grand pianos were at exams or festivals. He looked up at me with his sharp eyes and fearsomely bushy eyebrows and said, 'I see you are going to play a Chopin *Nocturne*. Let me hear it.'

I obligingly went to the piano, sat down, and completely blanked out. I couldn't even start the opening chords – and this was a piece I had just come first with in a piano competition. I looked up at him and said, 'I can't remember it.' (I always played by heart, and hadn't brought the music with me.) 'Perhaps,' I suggested, 'I'd better play a piece by Paradies,' (which I had taught myself, because I loved it).

'Very well,' he replied, and so I played the *Toccata* by Paradies – at top speed, I seem to remember.

The live televising was a few days later. Apart from allowing my mother to buy me a really pretty dress of blue-and-grey striped taffeta with a dark-blue velvet bodice, I wouldn't let her accompany me. (I told you I was stubborn.) This time, I was to go to Lime Grove Studios, not far from Shepherd's Bush. I knew exactly where these studios were – and this time, no one would waylay me!

Outside the studio, there was tension; children in tears or in a terrible state of nerves – mainly because their parents were in a state of nerves. That was why I hadn't allowed my mother to come with me. I didn't want anyone fussing me while I sat and tried to stay calm. There was a large, high, grey studio, hung about with metal gantries, ladders, cables, and gigantic lights pointing down. The make-up lady dabbed our faces with powder, and we watched as each child went in to be greeted by Huw Weldon – and did their bit. I don't think anyone disgraced themselves. Then my turn came. I walked through a door with a lighted sign which read *Broadcast in Progress*. I was on.

In between my last piano lesson, the interview, and then the transmission, I hadn't had a piano lesson, so my piano teacher settled in front of the television – as did all my friends – to see me in my moment of fame! She told me later how she nearly fell over backwards when, instead of the Chopin *Nocturne*, I played the *Toccata* by Paradies – as she had no idea I could play it. Huw Weldon then interviewed me and asked me what differences I saw between India and England, and I commented, among other things, that in India you would never see young girls with hair cut as short as boys, as you did here. I then played and sang one of my own songs out of *Red Shoes*, 'Am I Dreaming?' – and my moment of fame was over.

And it *was* a moment of fame. For months and months after, people would recognise me in the street or on a Tube, and say, 'Didn't I see you on the telly?' And I was on for hardly more than ten minutes!

But that episode – that first youthful brush with television – opened my eyes to a world I had never imagined existed. At that time, we still didn't have a television set, and my mother and sister had had to go to a neighbour's house to see me. I was thrilled by it! I loved the atmosphere, the idea of making programmes, and the interesting people. I thought it would be marvellous to be like Joanna Simons. But would any of this have happened if I had not met Lucy?

Nearly twenty-five years later, I had gone over to the town hall in Cheltenham with my children, to attend a concert given by Atarah's Band – Atarah, who I had barely seen since our school days. She didn't know I would be there. We had been out of touch for years and years – ever since

I left school. The hall was still empty when I arrived, and as I wandered in, suddenly there was Atarah! Still smiley and still bursting with enthusiasm. 'You?' she exclaimed incredulously. 'I was singing "Am I Dreaming?" in the car, all the way up from London.' It was as though she had materialised me out of the ether by singing my song out of *Red Shoes*.

You need to live a lifetime before you can look back and pinpoint all the people and events that were the major influences and turning points in your life: my grandfather, my mother, Lucy – and another school friend, Geraldine.

Chapter 8

Geraldine

She was three years older than me. People
assumed that if you liked an older girl, it must
be because you had a crush on her. I just
remember thinking what an interesting girl she
was. She had a way of walking, very controlled
and upright, and yet, I noticed, she always walked
up the main staircase from the school lobby two
steps at a time in a manner which was not
athletic, not bounding – but which almost made
her seem to glide. She had the strangest of green
eyes, and a long, pale face like a Modgliani
portrait. Once, when as a prefect she was on duty
at break, I went up to her and asked if I could be

her friend. To my surprise, she said yes. From then on, I often went to her house – a post-war council house on the outskirts of Ealing.

Where Lucy's mother and father flitted about like glorious birds in a world of stage lights, cameras and celebrity, and Lucy was a neglected little rich girl whose school shirts were often unchanged and black with the London grime of travelling a long distance to and from school, Geraldine's parents were modest. Her mother, she told me later, was 'sunken middle class' – probably like my grandfather – while her father worked on the Underground. But they were utterly devoted to the well-being of their children. Geraldine and her brother, Martin, would have been sent off to school in clean, ironed clothes, and returned to an immaculate house, with solid, nourishing meals which came on time and were set on the table. Somehow, unlike either my or Lucy's home, Geraldine's home exemplified the caring, nurturing, domestic family.

Again, I was taken in and nourished by them

too. Her mother loved music and always encouraged me to play their piano. I also remember her for being philosophical – something Geraldine must have inherited from her as, later, she went on to a profession in psychology. Because her parents lived in a council house the policy of the state dictated that, when they were approaching old age, they should move to a retirement council bungalow near the sea. I was aghast on their behalf. 'How cruel to make you move from the place which has been your home for twenty years; where you have all your friends and neighbours.' Her mother's rational and philosophical answer was: 'But now our children have grown up and left, we have no need of three bedrooms, and it is right that we should make way for a younger family who needs a home.' It was so logical and understanding, and was another nugget of wisdom for me to consider when trying to make sense of the world.

But as a schoolgirl Geraldine was a scholarship pupil; very intelligent and interested in all sorts of things quite out of my ken, though later she was to tell me that she, too, had not been happy at school, feeling that scholarship girls were discriminated against! Class snobbery was as devious and subversive as any other form of discrimination.

She loved French films and the cabaret music of Paris. Because of her, I admired Juliet Greco and Georges Brassens, loved listening to Edith Piaf, Charles Trenet and Josephine Baker. She loved the theatre as I did and it was with her that I was to see the first run of Samuel Beckett's *Waiting for Godot*; we spent a whole day queuing outside Covent Garden just to buy two gallery seats for the first appearance in London of the Bolshoi Ballet dancing *Romeo and Juliet*; and we went eagerly to see the Hungarian State Dance company when it visited.

Theatre and dance threatened to overtake my love of music. I spent long hours hanging around Questor's Theatre in Ealing, longing to help – if only to pick up fallen buttons in the costume department, and hang up the frocks. I had already, a year or two earlier, tried desperately to be in the London production of the musical *The King and I* set in Siam (modern-day Thailand). My mother had noticed an advertisement announcing that auditions were to be held at Drury Lane for children to take part in *The King and I*. I beseeched my mother to let me try. So the phone call was made (by me) and we duly presented ourselves at the stage door. It looked as if the whole of the Chinese community of London had turned up too (in lieu of there being a Thai community). Not only did they look right, but I was head and shoulders taller than they. Oh dear. But still – I had my moment of walking to the centre of the stage at Drury Lane, standing under a spotlight, and then proceeding out the other side. They told me kindly that I was too tall – and that was the end of my dream. But it was a wonderful experience, and only added to my fantasies of working in the theatre.

That Geraldine was going to study Psychology at university interested me very much. She always said she was more fascinated by people than anything else – and the subject was a study in

Ah yes – religion. For all the ecstasies I experienced through music, painting, theatre, and through my great love of nature, none of them was religious. Tears can flow just because of the combination of certain chords in music, just by the sound of a certain voice, or the sight of movement in a painting. I have felt so stirred by beauty, so riven with excitement, that I can feel my body rising almost into levitation. Perhaps the nearest I got to a religious experience was the first time I went to the Albert Hall as a school girl, to see a performance of Handel's *Messiah*.

Messiah is magnificent – not just for Handel's music, but because it makes you hear and emotionally comprehend every word, and the words from the King James Bible are beautiful. The effect of it was like a conversion – yet not a conversion to a faith, but conversion to the beauty of words and music. *Come unto me all ye that labour, and I will give you rest*. The messages are about peace and understanding, and threaded through with compassion. Yet I knew every time I listened to it, the one thing I wasn't feeling was a faith – and I felt deprived. I tried to feel it; tried to believe in God. I even had arguments with Him. 'Look,' I said, 'why don't you show me categorically that you exist, that miracles have happened, and can happen? And then I'll believe in you. If you are the Creator, the all-powerful, the all-knowing – why not stop the bad things: war, crime and hatred? Why be so elusive, so coy? Why not use your powers for good? Why not just show me?'

But He never did – and though I pursued my attempt to become a believer, and went to catechism classes and even got confirmed, I was never able simply to have a faith which was not based on rationality. However, I understand that there can be some beauty in pure faith: it might be like a distillation of all thought into one drop – like a drop of dew – which exists for itself, its only motive being to be itself; that when it falls it can inundate or nourish; that it has no moral value, and does not need to justify itself. Is that faith? If so, I can comprehend it without having it.

Perhaps because of my early years in India, my father's adulation of Mahatma Gandhi, and the visible presence of the poor all around us, I was bewildered and angered by the pomp and finery of the Church. Didn't Gandhi have it right when he insisted on dressing, eating and living as the poor do? Wasn't that what Christianity was supposed to be all about? Neither could I tolerate exclusivity. I saw and knew so many good people who weren't Christians: Hindus, Muslims, Sikhs and Parsees. The Christians themselves were so divided and competitive: the Anglicans, Catholics, Methodists, Seventh Day Adventists, Baptists, Mormons, and the Salvation Army. In the end, it seemed to me, there were good people and bad people; people who cared about others, and those who didn't. Their religion was as irrelevant to me as it was relevant to them. Now, although I love going into churches, and enjoy the architecture, the ceremonial, and the music – especially evensong – I still find myself gazing at the theatrical splendour and finding it at odds with what I understand Christianity to be about.

1. *The Queen's Coronation Procession, 1953*

*2. Lucy (right) with her sisters
and mother*

3. A 'prefab', built in about 1948

4. *Johannes Brahms, photographed in the 1850s*

5. *Geraldine*

6. *Atarah*

7. *Jamila (at the piano) and friends, with puppets, 1954*

8. *Jamila's brother, Philip, around 1960*

9. *Jamila's father, second from right*

10. *Jamila, her mother, sister Romie*

11. *Jamila at Le Manoir*

12. *Jamila skiing*

13. *Aldermaston to London march*

14. *Gladys Puttick and students*

15. *Jamila playing the piano, around 1960*

But I suppose that, somehow, all these accoutrements support 'faith', and that for many people faith is the most important aspect of their religion.

Once I went on a school trip to Switzerland. We went to a high mountain village and, when Sunday came round, were taken to a modest little church. I was astounded by its simplicity: bare whitewashed walls, plain wooden seats, and an altar which was barely more than a table, covered with a plain white cloth on which stood a simple crucifix. The pastor went through no rituals or ceremony that we were used to; he wore no rich embroidered robes, flaunted no gold chalice, or jewel-encrusted plates, but simply conducted a service which was of quiet prayer and a very intense sermon. Many of us came out moved – some in tears – and we were reflective in a way we had never experienced before.

At home, we all argued fiercely about religion, philosophy and politics. Debate was passionate. My mother read Alan Paton's book, *Cry the Beloved Country*, about the tragedy of the black predicament in South Africa. She was moved and motivated, and made us aware of the horrors of apartheid – as had Mr Hildebrand. It politicized me – and for years we would be boycotting South African goods until, at last, democracy came to that country in 1994 and the horrible system finally collapsed. Despite my mother's heavy workload, she went to evening classes to learn Russian, she joined the Civil Defence Corps and learned to drive ambulances. A few years later, with the founding of the Campaign For Nuclear Disarmament, we were to join her on the protest marches, walking all the way from Aldermaston's nuclear establishment to Trafalgar Square.

Chapter 9

The Family Reunites

After nearly three years of separation, my brother and then my father arrived to join us in England. Suddenly, the relative stability of the three of us, my mother, younger sister and me, was to be upturned.

My brother, Philip, was the first to come; by boat to Southampton, then train to Victoria then a taxi to Ealing. It was like meeting a stranger. He had grown so tall, was so dark and gangling and spoke with a pronounced Anglo-Indian accent. He had come to take his A Levels in England with the aim of going to university here. The very next day after his arrival, he too had to experience a new school and was soon plunged into relentless study. As he explained himself later, he arrived as an 'alpha male' used to being top in school. But now he found that he was way behind and needed to work harder than he'd ever done in his life.

The house was full of intensive study: me with piano practice and homework, Philip with mountains of study, catching up on all the subjects so alien to me at that time: Maths, Physics and Chemistry – no time for music, which was a pity, as he had been such a good violinist in Poona.

My so much younger sister, Romie, played 'school' with her dolls. She would line them all up and call out the register while my mother would be marking up papers and preparing her schoolwork for the next day. But every evening my sister and I waited eagerly at the piano for my mother to be free enough to accompany us singing together. Romie was now showing as keen a love of music as I had done. I loved the human voice; loved listening to lieder singers like

Elisabeth Schumann and Gerard Souzay. English singers like Kathleen Ferrier and Isobel Baillie were not just favourites of mine, but adored by the public, and I was always listening out for them singing duets together like *I Would that My Love* by Mendelssohn.

Then my father arrived. Suddenly a whole new dimension entered our lives. He had left education and become a civil servant of the new Government of India, and been appointed director of the new Tourist Office in London. His presence tipped us upside down. First of all, I could hardly admit to myself how embarrassing it was to have a father appear on the scene – especially one who was so different, so dark, so Indian. I felt confused and guilty at being deeply embarrassed. But there was his dynamism, his affection for us, his capacity for friendship and sociability, his fizzing energy with which none of us could keep up. My mother found herself having to attend cocktail parties, and be a hostess, and make small talk, and stand about with a glass of wine in her hand – something she was totally unused to and in which she had no interest.

But his affection and generosity had no bounds. We realised he would do anything for us – though he also seemed to believe that everyone was as generous and energetic and selfless as he was. Someone once said to me, 'I can't make out whether your father is an angel or a demon.' We in the family knew he was both.

With my father came more money. We soon acquired a television set and a car. Such luxuries! My father's work took him all over Europe, and he always reappeared with wonderful presents: sweaters from Norway, my first wristwatch (from Switzerland), perfume from France. He adored gadgets, and all sorts of things began to appear in the kitchen such as a potato peeler, a pressure cooker, an electric carving knife, a 'teasmade', and an endless stream of novelties. But the arrival of the tape-recorder he brought back from Germany provided another musical revelation for me. The German suppliers had left a demonstration tape on the machine with a recording of two bass arias from *The Magic Flute* by Mozart.

I was as bowled over as when I'd heard the Brahms Fourth Symphony, and played them incessantly. It took me into the world of Mozart, and he was to join the pantheon of my musical gods, along with Beethoven, Schubert and Brahms.

One angelic aspect of my father was his cooking. We began having wonderful meals. Indians love their food, and many Indian men who came to Britain without mothers and wives soon, out of desperation, took to cooking their beloved rice and curries. My mother had always loathed domesticity and had never learned to cook. Most of our meals came out of tins, or she made meat and vegetable stews which, while not being cordon bleu, were at least nutritious. But now our house was filled with the smells of spices going into curry, rice and dal, and – most beloved of all – was his remarkable ability to make parathas and pakoras.

He made friends easily, and seemed to stride through life full of confidence, though frequently with his family trailing behind in bewildered agitation. We never knew when he was going to turn up with a friend – or even just a passer-by he'd got into conversation with, and immediately set about providing them with a meal – something for which he became famous among our friends. He was to be my model for Grandpa Chatterji when in later years I began writing children's books.

His ingenuity in the kitchen was legendary. Show him a kitchen and he could produce a curry. He could turn anything into a curry: left-over meat or chicken, a potato, a carrot or a brussel sprout; a tin of tomatoes or a fading cabbage. So long as there was an onion in the house – an onion was compulsory – give him some oil, an odd packet of coriander and cumin seed, a pinch of salt, a sprinkle of black pepper, a bit of this and a bit of that, and it could all go into the pot and somehow emerge as a delicious dish. Got no rolling pin for rolling out a parathas? A milk bottle will do. Many of my friends thought a milk bottle was obligatory for rolling out parathas. Got no pastry cutter for cutting puris out of his rolled dough? No problem – a tin lid will do. But woe betide anyone who liked a tidy kitchen. Whenever my father took over a kitchen – and he has taken over kitchens all over Europe – it was as if a hurricane had hurtled through. The kitchen was his playground. However, he hated being cooked for, and deplored eating out in restaurants.

But one thing my father was hopeless at cooking was porridge. We always went to school on a bowl of porridge, but as the saucepan would sit on the stove unstirred, by the time we came to eat it, it was lumpy and horrible!

Our little house must have pulsated with the clamour of all of us – each trying to get on. Every morning was a frantic dash to gobble up our lumpy porridge and get away to school and work: my mother to the grammar school where she taught; my father into his office in central London; my young sister, needing to be dropped off at school in Acton – desperate not to be late. My brother was preparing for A Levels, and I was shredded in all directions, wanting to get involved in too much, none of it sufficiently to do with schoolwork, and O Levels hovering on the horizon.

My headmistress summoned me. She was perplexed. 'What exactly do you want to do in life?' she asked me.

'Music,' I answered. 'I'll be a composer or something.' It sounded hopelessly airy-fairy and impractical.

'You do realise,' she said, 'if you don't get at least five O Levels, you won't even be accepted into Trinity College of Music as a full-time student.'

That shook me. I promised to work. I dropped all my extras: all my hanging round Questor's Theatre, my lessons on the oboe and French horn – which I'd taken up along with folk dancing and choir – all my treasured activities that had made life at school bearable. I dropped everything except the piano, as I was about to take my Grade 8, and set about aiming to pass at least five O Levels.

It was the Music O Level I loved best. We had a good teacher who had already introduced me to new music which I would love for ever, like William Walton's *Belshazzar's Feast*. I can't even remember what we studied for those other O Level subjects: neither the books we learned for English, nor the period in History. But for Music we studied a movement of the Mozart *Clarinet Quintet*, and the overture to Wagner's *Die Meistersinger*. My mother took me to see this opera at the Royal Opera House, Covent Garden – my very first opera, five hours long – but perhaps because I had studied its themes and motives I sat through in a trance, and have loved it ever since.

It was to be my last year at school. Nothing would induce me to stay on and do A Levels, or consider going to university. I was fifteen, sixteen in August. I passed my Grade 8 and managed to get my five O Levels, and announced I was leaving school for ever.

I can fly. I am flying in the gym hall, bobbing up

Chapter 10

Sixteen, and
Never Been Kissed

It was 1956; a momentous year which was to define my political thinking. In July, the debates and arguments in my household raged about the Suez Canal in Egypt. Should Anthony Eden have taken the British troops into Suez to try and stop the Egyptian leader, Colonel Gamal Nasser, from nationalising the Suez Canal? This was to be yet another traumatic sign for the British people, that their Empire and its influence was in sharp decline; another sign that Britain was not invincible, that brown-skinned people were not inept and unable to run either countries or canals. The year would end with the brutal suppression by the Soviet Union of the Hungarian Uprising, which would cause many Communist sympathisers and intellectuals to reassess their political allegiances. As Suez raged, I left school for good. I thought I would go straight on to Trinity College of Music in London, where I had attended as a Junior Exhibitioner – but no. They didn't accept students until they were seventeen. I refused to stay on at school. 'I'd rather go and work in a factory for a year,' I cried. 'Or,' I suggested, 'could I not go to the Conservatoire de la Musique in Lausanne?'

On that school trip to Switzerland, we had spent a day in Lausanne, and I had hunted out the conservatoire and entered it. I had walked up those steps and through the front doors. No one stopped me, or asked who I was. I felt miraculously invisible, and wandered along the corridors listening to music seeping out of practice rooms: students having lessons, others practising; it was a cacophony of singers, pianists, violinists, clarinettists and flautists. I found an empty studio with a piano and sat down to play. I didn't feel an intruder, a stranger or a foreigner. I felt I was on my territory; this is where I should have been all my life – and where I now ought to be. I had always wished that I could have been at a music school instead of a conventional one. I knew that in some places, like Moscow, children entered a conservatoire from as early as nine years old, and music was the central focus of their lives rather than it being peripheral. I was sure that, had I been able to experience that kind of education, I would have thrived on it.

The thought germinated. To my joy, my parents told me that I was going to Lausanne. I would be enrolled in a school called Le Manoir, and attend the Lausanne Conservatoire of Musique.

'C'est si mal'
(sung to the tune of 'C'est si bon!' made famous by Jean Sablon)

D'habiter au Manoir
Nous mangeons pommes de terre
De matin jusqu'au soir

C'est si mal,
Nous n'avons des garçons
Nous n'avons la vie gai,
Mais toujours 'La Viret'.

Who was 'La Viret'?

She was the ferocious sister of Madame Decourvet, the principal of Le Manoir. Where her sister was slim and petite, with an armour-plated Parisian elegance, with never a hair out of place, and a chic to grace any salon, Madame Viret was short – though the word 'petite' would not describe her. She was dumpy, broader-boned, lacked chic, and didn't wear the tailored suits as Madame Decourvet did. Her bespectacled eyes glared at us with undisguised contempt from beneath her unkempt grey hair, which sprang from her head like a bush – and I felt she hated us. We hated and feared her. She was incredibly strong for an old lady, and would sometimes apprehend you with a vice-like grip on your arm.

These two ageing widows ran their school for girls with an iron rod. Reputation was everything. Lausanne and its environs were booming with international schools, finishing schools and all sorts of schools in between; all highly competitive; mostly, if not all, segregated – for boys or for girls. They dreaded having any smear on their institutions; any hint of romance, sex, secret liaisons or, worst disaster of all, a pregnancy, could bring down a school.

Soon after I had arrived, an older, bolder, rebellious American girl was seen in the town talking to boys in a Lausanne coffee shop, and on her return to school she was locked into a room. I sent outraged letters back to my mother. 'They've made her a prisoner!' But she was probably pleased that it proved there was discipline. The girl left soon after, but it set the repressive tone we were all to endure.

It was the first time I had ever left home – I hadn't even liked sleeping over at my friends' houses – so I was desperately homesick those first few weeks – a feeling I had never experienced before. But I soon made friends with girls I could never have imagined meeting in England: Aphrodite from Greece – a beautiful, sad, neglected rich girl who wrote poetry and thought about suicide, and who hadn't been home for two years because it hadn't suited her parents. There was friendly Ellen, an American from Alabama, who was modest and unpretentious and a loyal friend. There was Jessica, an English girl who played the cello; and there was Lynette, also English but from Bangkok, who looked like Rita Hayworth; terribly thin, terribly fashionable and obsessed with men.

Lynette and I formed a strange friendship. I never attempted to compete with her chic, or her desire to attract men, but I found her interesting and different. It's hard to know sometimes why one makes friends with this person and not that – but one of the teachers was worried by my association with her. It's true that I looked like a schoolgirl barely out of gymslips, while Lynette

110

looked like a film star. Perhaps she saw me as an innocent in the company of a virago! Yet maybe we were friends because I mothered Lynette, cared for her when she was sick, packed her trunk when she made a mess of it one holiday when she was returning to Thailand; that I was an easy companion who, for a while, allowed herself to be a kind of chaperone for her. But while she sat in cafés appraising men and angling herself to make an impression, I childishly savoured the far more sensuous reality of a Coupe Danmark – ice cream in a glass bowl, topped with fresh cream, and presented with a small silver jug of steaming hot chocolate, which I proceeded to pour into the centre. With what relish I watched the rivulets of hot chocolate trickle down like veins through the cream into the ice cream, scooping up heavenly mouthfuls with my silver spoon, mixing the chill with the hot.

But after some time, Lynette's obsessions became too restrictive for me – there seemed to be nothing else. I wondered what she wanted in life. I began to spend more time with Ellen, and finally decided to move rooms and be in one with her.

Lynette was devastated. I hadn't realised how much she had relied on me – and I hadn't realised how boarding school can build up such dependency on relationships. I hadn't meant it as a hostile act, but she never forgave me.

Le Manoir was a building in the old style: a large stone house with sloping roofs, turrets, and bay windows overlooking Lac Leman – where on the far shores, over that glorious ever-changing surface of the lake, we could gaze across to France.

The floors were wooden, and the main hall had a broad wooden staircase leading up to a gallery from which our bedrooms were situated. Each bedroom contained four or five beds, with their own lockers.

Below was the dining room, classroom and, most sacred of all, Madame Decourvet's salon – with French Louis Quinze-style sofas upholstered in satin, long brocade curtains, and a French chestnut-coloured grand piano – a Pleyal – on which I was frequently invited to play to entertain her guests.

Meanwhile, I was establishing my routines: regular piano practice, which I was allowed to do up in Madame Decourvet's eerily dark attic apartment on an upright piano tucked into a corner beneath a skylight, as well as attending lessons – all in French.

I went into the conservatoire twice a week: one visit for my piano lessons, and the other to study composition. This was about a twenty-minute trolley bus ride into town. It represented a joyful freedom, even though my piano teacher was a rigidly dry, unemotional, and stern man. I had played some Chopin to him as part of my admission interview into the conservatoire. It was the only time he ever complimented me. '*Elle joue du Chopin très bien*,' but from then on I struggled to please him. Although I had been reared on Czerny's piano exercises, and of course had pounded my way through all the scales and arpeggios – something you had to do for any exam – I had never experienced that close technical training so beloved by the French. 'Fingering, fingering!' he would wail, if I used a third finger instead of a fourth – and I would rebelliously wonder why it mattered if the sound was right. Why couldn't he say it was well played *even* if I put down the wrong finger? Music didn't seem to matter, only technique. It wasn't an easy relationship. After the gentle and constantly encouraging teaching of Jean Jukes and Gladys Puttick, he seemed like a heartless machine, and I felt like a beginner, in danger of losing confidence.

On the other hand, my composition teacher was a round, genial, roly-poly man with whom I learned harmony and counterpoint; who enjoyed Scottish and English folk songs, as I did, and who encouraged my composition. I learned how to read figured basses and write counterpoint. Our lessons were fun and informative.

Feeling frustrated with my piano lessons, I spent much time up in Madame Decourvet's attic apartment teaching myself the pieces I loved at that time – Chopin *Impromptus* and *Etudes* – and somehow we struggled on. I seemed to make progress despite my wayward fingering!

Madame Decourvet was an extraordinary snob. She only seemed to respect girls from the old European families; those of inherited wealth, and ancient genealogy. She too often despised the Americans and Germans, or those girls who were the daughters of businessmen. With her heavy tobacco voice, this little woman would peer over her desk, targeting one of these girls and, with a deep hissing and growling in her throat, would insult them, calling them '*Parvenue! Nouveau riche!* Rolling her French 'Rs' as if preparing a spit.

But Madame Decourvet often got me to play in her salon, especially requesting the two Brahms *Rhapsodies Op. 79*, which I had taught myself in England. Whatever problems I was having with my piano teacher, these proved I could play. Having no old European family heritage or aristocratic lineage to my name, she showed me off with pride like a butterfly she had collected.

With time, I grew to respect her. Madame Decourvet was a superb and passionate teacher. She believed in '*La Civilisation Française*'. Her French language classes were inspiring and logical, constantly able to show us the links between languages, making French so much easier to learn; and I will never forget her introducing us to *Le Grand Meaulnes*, the novel by Alain Fournier about love and obsession in a young boy moving from adolescence to manhood. Strange that she should so admire this book, yet be afraid of the adolescents in her school, and their growing awareness of love and feelings.

One of Madame Decourvet's missions was to civilise us, even if we were 'out of the bottom drawer'! Like all native French speakers – she was French Swiss – she believed there was only one true civilisation – and that was French. We were taken to concerts, theatres and exhibitions. We saw the greats, like the conductor, Pierre Monteux, and his Suisse Romande Orchestra, performing Stravinsky and Honneger, or one of my favourite pianists, Clara Haskill. Perhaps, I thought, I could be like her, playing Mozart – whose music was better suited to me than Brahms. We went to the theatre to see Moliere's *Tartuffe* by the famous French theatre company La Comedie Française, Yes – we were being educated and civilised.

But we also went on long walks into the woods around Lausanne, often stopping for refreshments at woodland chalets which served thick chunks of brown bread and honey, and mugs of steaming hot chocolate. We swam and boated, we skated and skied, and loved our weekly shopping excursions into the town.

But after our outings, at supper in the evening, Madame Decourvet would glare round the table at us all and ask, 'Who LOOKED at a boy today?' She meant it. She had a way of making you feel guilty even if you weren't.

Yet strangely, it was Madame Decourvet's own snobbery which led to my liaison with one of her prized guests at our '*Grand Dîner*' – the weekly dinner, when we had to dress up and learn how to be gracious guests and hosts! (This was the 'finishing' part of a finishing school – which nearly finished me off.)

Etienne was a young bachelor and a duke. Madame was in awe of anyone who was titled, and so he was a welcome visitor to Le Manoir. Somehow, Etienne and I got talking – perhaps after a *Grand Dîner*. Discreetly, he suggested that he meet me after my music lessons, and that instead of taking the trolley bus back to school he would drive me. We could use the time saved to take a walk by the lake.

I agreed. It was such a secret that I told no one – not even Ellen.

But this was not a steamy liaison or love affair. I had never had a boyfriend, and hadn't even entered that world yet, of boy talk and boy-friends. At sixteen, most of my English school friends hadn't entered that world either. It wasn't simply my innocence; it was the times. We weren't surrounded at every turn by billboards, advertisements, television, film – and the whole industry of commercialised sex. In any case, I was far too preoccupied with school and music, and I had never met any boys, for this to be an issue. So it didn't even occur to me that Etienne and I were anything more than friends – even if it was a forbidden friendship.

Twice a week, his white Mercedes would be waiting for me outside the conservatoire. In the time it would have taken me to go back by trolley bus, he drove me down to the lakeside where we would talk and talk.

Why did Etienne never cross the line? Why did we never even kiss or cuddle? True, he was the most courteous and gentlemanly man I ever met. Was it because he wondered whether he could, or should, fall in love with someone like me – someone not of his religion, class or race? At twenty-eight years old, he was probably thinking about marriage. If so, I'm sure he would have expected virginity and propriety in his future wife. This was the Fifties, where respectability ruled, and sex before marriage was barely thinkable for a 'respectable' girl. Was it because I was only sixteen, and he was totally responsible and simply wouldn't take advantage? He would have valued his own reputation and family name. The most he ever did to show his affection was to put a loose arm around me as we sat in his car overlooking the lake, and gently stroke my neck.

I felt I became a sounding board for his questions – doubts even. We talked about the ways of the world, philosophy and religion. He was a Catholic, but asked my opinion about so many of its beliefs and dogmas: did I believe in birth control? (He was aware of the burgeoning world population and thought perhaps it was necessary.) Did I believe in transubstantiation – that the bread and wine offered at Holy Communion became the body and blood of Jesus Christ not symbolically, but literally? Did I believe in the Virgin birth and the Resurrection? Although I knew he was questioning and challenging his own religion, he was probably looking for a wife who could at least pay lip service to basic Catholic doctrine, and it must have become clear that I could not. He was fascinated by other religions and asked me about Hinduism, and the value of other faiths. Perhaps he wondered whether non-Catholics really were condemned to hell if they were not converted. I had by now encountered a number of different faiths, most of which believed that others not of that faith were condemned to hell – something I found incompatible with belief in a merciful God. So if I felt that Etienne was assessing what qualities he should look for in a future wife, I also felt he was trying to assess the beliefs he had been brought up with, against those he was developing for himself.

For my part, I had no designs on Etienne. Looking for a husband was not even in my mind-set – only study, and the years ahead of working to become a musician. Perhaps he sensed that, and he felt unthreatened too, for I would surely not be acceptable as the wife of a duke, linked to one of the oldest royal families in Europe. He called me his '*petite philosophe*' (little philosopher), and that's how it stayed.

But if I arrived in Lausanne a complete

innocent, it was not Etienne who destroyed it –
even in my mind. He was as far removed from
that as film stars and literary heroes, and the
unreal romance of fiction and Hollywood
movies. It was the American girls who opened my
eyes to everything.

They considered themselves far more mature
than their European counterparts; they drove
cars, were aware of fashion, and talked sex and
marriage. Men and boys were discussed
incessantly. It seemed very important to them,
from a far earlier age than in Europe, to have a
boyfriend – to be spoken for. It was as though life
was just one big preparation for their wedding
day – though I never heard talk of any life beyond
that. They didn't talk of jobs, or even of children.
Every night they plastered their faces with night
creams and twisted their hair into rollers. I
wondered how they could possibly sleep – and
would they continue this practice when they were
married? They shaved their arms and legs, and
perfumed their bodies with deodorants and skin
tonics. Their talk was alien to me: men were

discussed, analysed and debated; their sexuality trawled over as they were categorized into hunks and pansies – neither term which had been known to me. I learned about lesbianism and homosexuality in those intense conversations, often at night after lights out. Their judgements were lethal. No wonder I never even mentioned Etienne.

But it was in that year that I had my first proposal. Yes, stereotypically it was from my ski instructor in Austria. That winter, when everyone from Le Manoir went somewhere for the winter holidays, my mother had the idea of sending me to a *pension* (a small family-run hotel) in Austria, where we had spent many happy summer holidays. We knew the family in charge, and she was confident that I would be well looked after.

I was enrolled into the ski school and found myself in a class being taught by Hermann.

I took to skiing like a duck to water. Soon I was doing all the runs – even the black ones.

I have a passion for speed. I had never experienced such exhilaration – except in dreams

– as when flying down a ski slope. I was rash and impetuous – completely unafraid. Yet these were the days of wooden skis, and ski boots which were strapped to the skis with no safety release if you fell. Broken legs and ankles were commonplace. But I was lucky – and continued to be lucky up until now (I tempt fate) – I still ski and am still addicted to speed.

How I loved observing the grace and style of the good skiers, in the same way that I am fascinated by the beauty and skill of the human body. It's why I loved skating and dancing, and watching athletes: I love the way the body is balanced; that it has to find a rhythm to negotiate the twists and turns of the ice or the piste; to be tuned up, pitched like a violin string, in a state of anticipation, and prepared for performance as well as the unexpected.

I always tried to ski as close behind Hermann as possible, to imitate his rhythmic swing and pace. Day by day, I gained in confidence – we all did in my class, and were soon being taken higher and higher up the mountain, from the blue runs to the red runs; and by the second week negotiating the black runs. I have never experienced such ecstatic terror as when skiing out of the chair lift at the top of the Valluga in St Anton. It was like being deposited inside the rim of a giant cup. There was no time to pause and look at the scenery; once you had glided off the chair, you had to ski or go into a fearful tumble; you had to concentrate on everything you had been taught in the past week: bend the knees, lean *out* – '*Tal, tal*' (valley) the instructors would shout as they goaded you against your instincts, to lean out into the valley and away from the mountain.

I still feel that intense thrill every time I sit in a chair lift and am suddenly lifted above the clamour of crowds waiting in the queue, and there is that alpine silence, broken only by the swish of the cable. Now is the time for contemplation; to look at the beauty of the mountains with whom you are building up a relationship; you will ski their slopes, try and understand their terrain; you will study the skies

– sometimes hard blue, promising a day so hot you may ski in a T-shirt, or shifting grey with an intimation of snowfall, when the visibility can turn to white-out, and there can be all the anxiety of avoiding a fall.

Towards the end of my two weeks, Hermann had become smitten with me. One evening after a dance in the town, he kissed me full on the lips, pushing his tongue into my mouth – something I had no idea people did! I rushed back to my room and swilled out my mouth several times. Now I come to think of if – my first kiss! But he didn't disgust me. I liked him a lot – but not romantically. I thought this was just a bit of bold flirtation, but no, the next time we met off the slopes he begged me to marry him.

'I can't possibly!' I exclaimed. 'I couldn't study music up here in the Alps!'

He was heartbroken, and wept. This was another lesson I learned about the sensitivity of people's feelings.

Chapter 11

Even Ellen

I returned to Le Manoir from my skiing holiday older and, if not wiser, knowing a little more about the world. Until then I had been a child, tossed between India and England, tossed between their politics, fate and cultures; between the small-scale concerns of homes, schools and friendships, and the big scale of global events like Indian Independence, Partition, war and its aftermath. But I had no real sense of my place in the world or quite where I was going to fit in – nor did I even think about it. I came back from skiing to find democratic Europe reeling from the aftermath of the Hungarian Uprising and coping with the thousands of refugees, many of them young students, who had fled from Hungary. The Hungarians had tried to throw off the repressive yoke of the Soviet Union with catastrophic consequences. Hundreds were shot in the streets, or hung from the lampposts. Many Swiss families took them into their homes. I met a young bewildered student called Tibor struggling to learn French and work out what his future would be; he was bemused by my passion for Bartok and Hungarian folk music, when all he wanted to listen to was American rock and roll!

My next goal was just six months away – to gain a piano scholarship into Trinity College of Music, and I spent hours up in Madame Decourvet's upper apartment practising till darkness filled up the room, leaving me in a solitary spotlight from the lamp on top of the piano.

In Switzerland, I had been confronted with more of the world than I had ever known: Europe, South Africa and America. I was seeing and hearing at first hand other differences in culture, religion, attitudes and aspirations. I met Mormons for the first time and learned a bit about some of their beliefs, which were based on some ancient texts – plates – written by a prophet called Mormon, which their founder, Joseph Smith Jr, claimed to have translated with the help of God. Some believed in polygamy, and that they were the restoration of latter-day Christianity. I realised that people could hold the oddest beliefs and yet still be some of the kindest people I had ever met.

But though I found it easier to take on board people's religious beliefs – after all, I had been doing that all my life – I found it harder to be tolerant of people's political views. I argued bitterly with the white South African girls about apartheid when they expressed the views they had been brought up with – that the blacks of South Africa had not yet evolved to the same state of development as the whites: that they had just 'fallen out of the trees', and so could not be treated as equals. They denied they hated blacks. 'I love my black nanny!' protested one girl.

'What do you mean by love?' I challenged. 'Do you love her enough to let her live in the same street as you? Do you love her enough to let her sit on the same bench as you, or ride in the same bus?'

She was silent – perhaps she had never had her culture and beliefs challenged before. 'Well, why don't you go over there and do something, if you feel so strongly,' she retorted finally.

'What, me?' I cried, holding out my brown hands.

I think we both realised simultaneously that she had forgotten completely that I was non-white. By her terminology, I was 'a coloured' – and we wouldn't even be speaking to each other if we were in South Africa.

But this was to be a familiar experience – people forgetting my colour. Even Ellen thought of me as white – which only goes to prove that colour is skin deep, and that it rapidly becomes insignificant when other more important attributes take over.

Even Ellen!

We were once shopping in the town when suddenly she stopped dead and almost burst into tears. She had overheard the familiar Alabama drawl. The voices were round the corner in the arcade. I expected Ellen to rush over and introduce herself, but instead she hung back, listening, longing to speak to her fellow countrymen, but paralysed.

'Go and speak to them, Ellen,' I begged her. 'They'd love to meet you.'

'I can't! I can't!' she cried regretfully.

'But why?' I simply didn't understand.

'Because they're black!' she said.

I was shocked. I had never met this kind of barrier before; first the South Africans, and now Ellen! I argued with her. 'Why should that matter? They're from your home town. What harm can it do just to say hello?'

'You don't understand,' she replied. 'My grandmother owned slaves.'

She was homesick and confused. I didn't pester her with questions. Perhaps I was unwilling to lose her friendship, though I wanted to ask her:

Why did it matter that her grandmother had once owned slaves? Why should it matter that black people in America had once been slaves? They were free now; equally human; truly American: How did Ellen's attitude differ from the South Africans'? Of course, I didn't understand the extent of the bitterness and brutality which still existed in the American South; I didn't know that segregation was as absolute there as in South Africa. The American Civil Rights Movement hadn't even started. The stand-off at Little Rock was still to come.

These arguments and debates, especially with people like Ellen from the deep American South, and with the South African girls, made me realise how complex life was. It made me reappraise words like 'prejudice'. They each felt deep feelings of kinship and even love for black people – but I realised that the love was no more than the love one has for an animal or pet. They were repelled by the thought of black people being the same as they were, as human as they were. What they had was not a simple prejudice, but a belief.

They believed – as one believes that the moon is in the sky – that black people were inferior. They believed it as much as people in Christendom before Galileo believed that the sun revolved around the earth and not vice versa. It was so ignorant, so ingrained. Yet those who were my friends I could not suddenly treat as enemies. If they had the confusion of liking me and wanting to be my friend, even though it would be unacceptable in their own cultures, I had the confusion of really liking people who stood for things that were completely against my own interests and principles.

But debates about religion and politics were not nearly so prevalent as evidence of '*Civilisation Americaine*' which filtered through the school. From some rooms came the sound of Elvis Presley, Billy Haley and teenage boy stars with voices still cracking with adolescence, like Paul Anka and the Everly Brothers. The North Americans rocked and rolled and bebopped, in their swinging skirts and bobby socks; but from another room, down the corridor, came the sound of the tango, the rumba and the cha-cha played by the South American girls from Brazil, Venezuela and Costa Rica. Each group stuck fiercely, almost nationalistically, to their own music – a foretaste of the scenes to come in the musical *West Side Story*. I noticed that though they belonged to the same continent, there were no friendships that I saw between North and South Americans – except for one wonderful Venezuelan girl, of exceptional beauty and intelligence, called Marianna. She seemed more mature than the rest of us, but occasionally enjoyed entering into our wide-ranging conversations and participating in our debates – usually to make us see how petty and paltry some of our views were. She was reading Hemingway and John Steinbeck, and it was she who introduced me to American literature and poetry. Our brief encounter left its mark!

But the Americans played more than rock and roll music.

This was the age of the musical – and each new one, whether from Rogers and Hammerstein, or

Lerner and Loewe, was awaited with excited anticipation. Often we knew one or two songs which had been released ahead of the production, and played on the radio – so it created an even greater expectation.

I was in love with the American musical. My sister and I had all those vinyl LPs of *Oklahoma, Carousel, The King and I* and *South Pacific*. We had learned them, every one, until we were note perfect and word perfect. When Ellen came back from her Christmas holiday in America, she brought me a recording of *My Fair Lady* ahead of the production coming to London. I was enchanted, and soon knew every word and note of that too.

But for me, more stirring than Elvis, rock and roll, or even the musical was my discovery of 'black music' such as Little Richard, Fats Domino, Ray Charles, Duke Ellington, Louis Armstrong and Satchmo. Their rhythmic energy and searing emotion seemed to enter my bloodstream.

My mother had adored the voice of Paul Robeson, the black American singer, and I did too. We had his records and learned songs like 'Swing Low Sweet Chariot', 'Steal Away', 'Lindy Lou', and 'Take Me Away from the River'. He travelled all over Europe giving recitals to packed houses, and spreading abroad the beauty and power of the 'negro spiritual'. These songs had a moral and religious compulsion about them as did Handel's *Messiah* – though they were despairing, often expressing a longing for death to release them from the pain of their lives. Once Robeson sang at the Royal Albert Hall, and my mother took me to see him. We even hung about the stage door afterwards, being pushed about in a seething, devoted and determined mob, desperate to touch him and get his autograph.

There was to be another eye-opener. When I told Ellen I had seen Paul Robeson, and how much I loved his singing, she looked puzzled. 'Who's he?' she asked.

I was incredulous. 'He's a black American singer – from your part of the world. He sings spirituals. He's wonderful, and absolutely everyone knows his name in England. How could you not have heard of him?'

But she shook her head adamantly. 'Never heard of him!'

I thought about this. How could she not know him? It was like an English girl saying she'd never heard of Winston Churchill. It seemed so extraordinary. There must be an explanation. Then I remembered that he had become a member of the Communist Party – and this at a time when America was consumed by fear and loathing of Communism, when Joseph McCarthy, a senator in the Eisenhower government, was conducting witch hunts identifying Communists and their sympathisers, and hunting down anyone deemed 'unAmerican'! It was a time when people lost their jobs, were black-listed, and made unemployable for years. Some went to prison. Paul Robeson had been classified 'unAmerican' and had his passport removed from him. I remember my anguish. How could they call *him* unAmerican. To me he represented everything I loved about America. But so successfully had they turned him into a non-person, that Ellen from the deep South – who should have known all these songs – had never heard of him.

'He is a Communist,' I told her.

'Oh well!' she replied with disgust. 'No wonder I haven't heard of him.'

I was learning fast; Communism in America was despised and virtually a criminal offence, whereas in Europe it was an ideology, respected and adhered to by many. It was often at the heart of the huge philosophical and political debates which raged in universities and the workplace, in the press and in books. It affected your attitudes to do with the future structure of society; the welfare state, education, health and workplace practices – trade unionism. People were then so polarised that if they said they were Labour or Conservative, Socialist or Communist, you knew immediately what many of their other attitudes were too. Winston Churchill had talked about an Iron Curtain coming down after the Second World War: an invisible, yet impenetrable barrier which divided the western democracies from Russia and the eastern bloc countries it had sucked into its grip, like Hungary, Poland, East Germany and Czechoslovakia. The Iron Curtain personified Cold War politics; the icy ideological divide between right and left, capitalism versus Communism, American and western democracies versus the USSR and one-party states. Each side had nuclear weapons, and each side brandished them menacingly. Every other country in the world needed to know which side they were on. Things were brutally simple and clear – or so we thought – as clear as War or Peace, Life or Death: this side of the Iron Curtain or the other.

In the 1950s, at the peak of the Cold War, there was real unease, as we knew perfectly well what the consequences of a nuclear war would be. People had seen what had happened when the bomb was dropped on Hiroshima and Nagasaki at the end of the Second World War.

People were violently polarised between those who felt a nuclear deterrent was essential for the country's security, and those who felt that any such security was an illusion, and that the sheer immorality of making weapons of mass destruction was unacceptable. When the Campaign For Nuclear Disarmament (CND) was founded in 1957, many opposed it, believing that its members were tantamount to traitors; that the organization was being used by Communists and the Soviet Union, and infiltrated with spies and agitators. I became a member of CND soon after it was founded. How we scorned government suggestions that we could survive a nuclear strike by blackening our windows, stocking our cellars with food and water, and putting paper bags over our heads!

I returned to England for the Easter holidays, and took part in the first CND march from Aldermaston to Trafalgar Square. It was led by a senior churchman, Canon Collins, the philosopher Bertrand Russell, and the politician Michael Foot – people whose integrity and morality I could not possibly suspect. These were not rabble-rousers. They were more like Old

Testament prophets, warning of doom if we didn't change our policies. The march was made up of mothers pushing babies, grannies and grandpas, elderly soldiers, people who had experienced the war – some of them two world wars; there were vicars, students, university professors, poets and writers and scientists; but yes, there were also leftist politicians, trade unionists and Communists who – according to the right-wing political groups, were Soviet sympathisers who ought to be loathed as if they were traitors – and so the country was polarised. Some people spat and jeered at us as we walked by, others handed out refreshments and words of encouragement. To some, we were simple-minded stooges of evil manipulators from behind the Iron Curtain. To others we were heroic. I met Igor on the march; perhaps his name indicated some kind of Russian blood in his veins, but for all that, he was an English public-school boy, a Catholic, whose father worked for MI5. The cause for him was about morality, and was logical.

CND was to continue throughout the coming decades; throughout the horrors of bloody wars in Vietnam and Cambodia, and through the terrors of the Cuban Missile Crisis (when the USA and the USSR teetered on the brink of possible nuclear war). It lasted into the Seventies, and the determined siege by the women in the protest camp at the Greenham Common nuclear base in Berkshire, which lasted years. Even if by that time the nuclear arms debate was a lost cause, who could say they were wrong to try? Perhaps we were naive to believe in human nature. Perhaps the bomb, once out of Pandora's box, could never be put back. In the light of that truism, perhaps Britain could never have given up the bomb unilaterally. Yet for all that, neither is there any proof that Britain's possession of the bomb did anything for world peace, but simply legitimised it for other countries too. The argument is, alas, hypothetical.

Chapter 12

Back to Face the Future

It was only one year in my life, that year in Lausanne, but with all the intensity of ten. I shall never forget my friends, too many of them poor little rich girls, deeply depressed and unhappy, spending months – sometimes years – away from their families and parents, emotionally neglected; like beautiful Aphrodite who wrote tragic poetry and thought about suicide; like Nina from Brazil, probably anorexic, who got thinner and thinner, who sat at the dining table with silent tears rolling down her cheeks; and her friend Marcia, so much the opposite from her, who was always hungry and gobbled down everything she could, who was greedy, yet kind, and tried hard to comfort and encourage Nina. Happiness could not be bought.

I learned how to leave childhood and confront the adult world. I learned a sense of dress and noticed fashion. I wore the long, almost ankle-length dresses, flounced out with huge layers of net petticoat. I easily slid into the sheath dress, slim-fitting and figure-clinging. On a holiday back to England I had been to visit Mr Hildebrand, and saw his eyebrows rise. 'You've become a woman,' he said softly.

Yes – I too began wearing make-up, getting my hair done, and shaving my legs and under my arms – this last practice leading to an ignominious end to my year at Le Manoir.

Back at school for my last term, I developed a boil under my arm. Madame Decourvet was unsympathetic. 'It's because you've been shaving under your arms,' she declared accusingly. Strangely, my English friend, Jessica, also simultaneously developed boils under her arms.

Madame Decourvet insisted that we must have shared razors, even though we knew this wasn't possible. We didn't even sleep on the same floor. Finding us responsible for our own misfortune seemed to mean that we must pay the penalty and take the consequences, so no help, let alone sympathy, was forthcoming.

We both suffered agonies, but Jessica's boils at last cleared up. Mine went from bad to worse, and soon I was sleepless with pain. We had an ancient *gouvernante* – a matron whose job was to care for us – but she was deeply unsympathetic. She had no rapport with any of us. We teased her mercilessly, this poor woman, who, I fear was completely out of her depth with us wilful, highly emotional and volatile girls. I presume it was she who arranged for a nurse to come and administer penicillin to me because an even more ancient, bent lady appeared one day. She opened her medical bag and, with claw-like hands, drew out a huge syringe with a very thick needle. She ordered me to bend over while, with an exceedingly shaky hand, she proceeded to plunge the needle into my buttock. I was delirious after this injection, and after each of several more which she delivered over a period of a week. Perhaps I was allergic to penicillin. No one asked. The boils got worse – and I was frantic. I paced the corridors, hunched in agony. Finally, in desperation, I rang my father, who I knew was spending a period looking after the Paris office. 'Please give me permission to leave immediately,' I begged, which he duly did, as term was almost at an end anyway.

Madame Decourvet was outraged. 'I suppose you cried on the telephone,' she sneered. (Why did she always think the worst of her girls?)

'No I didn't,' I retorted. 'But I told him I must see a doctor!'

'Let me see these boils,' she demanded – no, she hadn't taken the trouble to look before.

I showed her. It was not a pretty sight – and she fell silent.

That night, there was to be one more *Grand Dîner*. I hadn't seen Etienne for a while, because I was so incapacitated. I knew he was coming, and felt deeply sad that I wouldn't have the chance to say goodbye properly. As he came into the hall I leaned over the balcony and managed to explain I was unwell. He waved. There was nothing else he could do, and that was the last time I saw him.

The next day I packed my belongings, was escorted to Lausanne station, and put on a train to Paris. It was the final end of my school days.

My angel-demon father was there waiting for me at the Gare du Nord. My dear father, so willing to do anything for people – yet, as in my mother's case, unable to comprehend physical suffering. He had organised a doctor's appointment, but this was followed straight after by a large cocktail party which he wanted me to attend. There was nothing he loved more than showing off his children.

The cocktail party was full Parisian chic; men in shining dark suits and silk ties, elegant women with fabulously coiffured hair, their dresses of French haute couture, holding fluted wine glasses in one hand, smoking cigarettes with the other (through long, bone cigarette holders, as Audrey Hepburn was to do in the film *Breakfast at Tiffany's*) looking like exotic birds with strange beaks. But my father outclassed them all, as handsome and elegant as an Indian prince in his official Indian dress, which consisted of white, jodhpur pyjamas, and a raw-silk black jacket, buttoned up to a Nehru-style collar at the neck, and falling away to mid-calf. I should have matched him and worn a sari, but I wasn't used to it, so I wore one of my elegant sheath dresses and hoped I looked sophisticated. But I didn't feel it. While they mingled, smoked and drank, and chattered their small talk, the painkiller I had been given gradually wore off, and I began to wilt miserably, wishing my father would notice and take me away.

As a postscript to my year away – my gap year, as it could be termed today – I recall one final lesson from those times. One of the skiers in my ski-school class in St Anton was an American; to my mind, a youthful but distinctly middle-aged man called Bob, with a French wife who had stayed down in a lower-level ski class. He was fun. We joked and larked about a lot – both of us thoroughly enjoying each other's company on the ski slopes. When the fortnight ended, he gave me his card and warmly invited me to visit him and his wife should I ever be in Paris. I knew it was a genuine invitation.

Finding myself in Paris now, I suggested to my father that we look up Bob. I had his card, so we telephoned, and he invited us both to tea. He lived quite a way out of Paris, in a leafy almost rural suburb, in a large rambling house. After a not inconsiderable journey we arrived, me certain that it would be to a warm and jocular reception. But, greeted at the door by Bob, I realised the atmosphere was distinctly frosty. With great difficulty, we endured about two hours with Bob and his wife, playing table tennis, drinking tea, and trying vainly to make conversation. All Bob's humour of our skiing days was completely absent. He looked strained and uncomfortable, while his wife could barely bring herself to engage with us at all.

As soon as courtesies allowed, my father and I extended our heartfelt thanks for the tea, and left. He and I never discussed what could have been the reason for our barely civil treatment. Why? Was this the holiday friendship syndrome: fun at the time, but unwelcome back home? Could it be because his wife was jealous of me? It didn't seem possible. Perhaps, like Ellen, Bob had been colour-blind with me, but seeing me arrive with my very dark-skinned father, he realised that we were 'coloured' – and therefore unacceptable. I'm not sure what lesson it taught me, except to be wary of following up on passing holiday acquaintances – even those as nice as Bob.

Practising up in Madame Decourvet's garret sitting room, I had been preparing the Chopin *Etude in G flat major Op. 10 No. 5* known as *The Black Note Etude*, for my scholarship to Trinity College. I was to perform before an examining board on my return to London.

Leaving my father in Paris, I took the train and ferry, journeying back to Ealing and the little terraced house my mother had by now bought.

I plunged straight back into intense practice, and was duly awarded my scholarship. Strangely, it was a mixed blessing. The scholarship paid for my tuition but nothing else, as I lived in London. Our family finances were now so improved that I was not entitled to any added grant from the local authority, and my parents refused to give me enough money to move into digs. They were right, of course; what digs would endure the sound of six or seven hours' piano practice a day? But I had grown up, become independent; yet suddenly, I was a child again in my mother's eyes. She exerted her authority over me as if I might somehow be abducted to the land of Sodom and Gomorrah. She became strict to the point of paranoia, trying to control my life, my where-abouts and even my bedtime. It was to be the start of a strained relationship, where she seemed unable to enjoy her teenage children, but simply suffered huge anxiety and disproportionate fears

black trousers, black, long Victorian jacket, and a black top hat. He was followed by a woman also completely in black, wearing a full, hooped skirt, with a shawl round her shoulders and a peaked black bonnet tied with a ribbon under her chin. They walked past the bottom of my bed.

'Was that you playing the piano?' I asked curiously.

The man didn't pause but continued walking, and disappeared straight through the wall opposite. The woman stopped and turned to look at me – except she had no face. My whole being shuddered in terror as she, too, then walked through the wall and vanished.

Chapter 13

Ne'er the Twain Shall Meet

At that time, people used to wag their heads and pontificate generally about "mixed marriages', and how they were certain they couldn't work. The reasons usually put forward were because of cultural differences. But I knew that, in the case of my parents, cultural difference wasn't the cause. Culturally, they were amazingly similar. The strain on them was quite simply colour. It was colour prejudice which was destroying them.

My mother suffered the most – and was the one to regret her marriage. Her regret made her lurch into a kind of denial of who she was, of the decisions she'd made in her life, and even who her children were. On the one hand she loved us, yet on the other she wished we were white enough to be indisputably English. I never doubted her love and maternal defence of us, yet now, in England, it was as if she couldn't accept us for what we were. It began to distort her political views. From being the radical-thinking avant-gardist in the family; the first political protester; the doer, the thinker; the one who made us aware of apartheid, nuclear weapons, and world politics now, to our horror and disbelief, she began to lurch so far right she even started being an apologist for apartheid in South Africa, and to believe that Kipling's chant *East is East and West is West and ne 'er the twain shall meet* was perhaps right after all. She went into a hard-line re-conversion; a recantation, back to Empire, back to the old racist beliefs. *Mea culpa* must have screamed in her breast.

Yet she was wrong. The 'twain' had met very well. Her problems were never cultural. My father had never expected her to be a demure Indian-style wife, trailing seven paces behind him. They were both educated, shared the same Christian values (my father was actually more of a committed Christian than she), and although the term 'feminism' was still not much discussed, my mother exemplified feminism, and my father, the 'modern man'. She continued her profession as a teacher, a working wife – something quite rare among the middle classes – and my father was only too happy to share domestic chores: cooking, shopping and cleaning. The stress which was finally bending and distorting this wonderful, intelligent, brave woman was colour prejudice – though she couldn't or wouldn't articulate it, and stay onside with us.

I don't know what taunts and snubs she must have endured. She never told us – though I know she suffered a series of anonymous telephone calls, which I now realise were abusive. Did all this erode her self-respect, somehow bring about this change? Did she feel it intolerable to be rejected by her own beloved people? She was as passionately English as my father was Indian.

What she couldn't defend in herself, or be proud of, was that she was ahead of her time – ahead of her time as a woman, as well as a moral being. Yes, she had broken racial taboos – but it was the taboos which were wrong, not her. Her defensiveness made her aggressive and contradictory, and her rejection of my father was confusing and, at times, cruel. My rejection of her changing views distressed her. She and I had always been an entity; the perfect relationship: mother and child, teacher and pupil. She had taught me everything up until then. But now my adored mother had become my adversary – even my enemy. With such tensions at home I now began life as a music student in London.

Despite my differences with my piano teacher in Lausanne, I had managed to progress. The proof was surely in getting a scholarship. I was now highly ambitious. The college mapped out a performer's course for me, believing me to have the qualities for a concert pianist, though this was not an ambition I had ever particularly entertained. But my love of music meant that I wanted to charge ahead and learn more and more repertoire. I had hoped to study with Gladys Puttick, but the college thought I should be in the hands of a professional pianist – one already in the concert world. It was to be a disaster.

Perhaps I was too much like my mother: self-willed, independent, even arrogant. If others didn't understand the goals I had set myself, I went along and tried to achieve them anyway. Just as I had lost the support of my music teacher at school over *Red Shoes*, so I lost the support of my piano professor at Trinity. She wanted to hold me back; teach me more thoroughly and more slowly. And I did learn from her: vital lessons – particularly in the playing of classical music like Bach and Mozart. She taught me the real value of notes – to really respect the differences in weight between quavers, semi-quavers and crotchets; the rests and the phrasing, tempo and rhythm. What she taught me, I took on board and never forgot. I know that they were some of the most important piano lessons I ever had. I believe she was a marvellous teacher in so many ways, and yet, I felt she was trying to break me in – like a wild horse needs breaking in. But my wildness was part of who I was, and just as a wild and wilful horse refuses its rider and tries to break down the fences holding it in, so I lurched and bucked and tried to gallop away.

It was more than two years since I had taken my Grade 8. I had made quite substantial technical progress since then, and I assumed I would go straight into taking the next exam, my Licentiate diploma, but she was against it and refused to endorse me. I entered myself, learned the music myself, and failed. It was the first time I had ever failed in music. I was devastated and humiliated. I tried again – and failed again. I couldn't do it on my own.

I plunged myself into drama. Instead of keeping up my second instrument, the violin, I had chosen to study drama as my second subject – and Trinity College in those days had a wonderful drama department, for the sake of its opera singers. It was run by a dynamic and charismatic woman, Pamela Barnard, who became a great source of inspiration for me. With her, I studied poetry and plays; learned to love Gerard Manley Hopkins, T. S. Eliot, Sean O'Casey and Eugene O'Neil. I took part in productions, acting in plays and stage-managing operas. I took and passed drama exams with LAMDA (the London Academy of Music and Drama), getting my Acting Gold Medal and Associate diploma, performing speeches by Shakespeare and Tennessee Williams.

My piano playing was in turmoil, but I was in turmoil too – and finally I cracked. People didn't talk much about nervous breakdowns in those days, not as much as now. But I realise in retrospect that I was on the edge of one. I began crying helplessly one day, and when Pamela Barnard asked me the cause of my distress I realised it wasn't my music. It was, as I blurted out, because my parents were quarrelling so bitterly.

But it was more than that. I was hurtling round

like a pilotless spaceship. I had no one to advise me, counsel me, put things into perspective; help me to see what was in my best interests. I was squandering my energies.

At my lowest ebb, my father announced that we were all going to go on holiday to India – the whole family, returning together after five years.

At one of my father's cocktail parties I had met a woman who worked at the BBC as a studio manager. She told me how she had taken a tape-recorder to India and made lots of recordings for the BBC archive. When I exclaimed with envy, 'Oh, I'd like to do that,' she gave me the name of the producer for whom she had worked.

I now telephoned the number and was invited to Broadcasting House to meet this producer. I described the journey we were going to make, from Delhi to Allahabad – my father's family home – on to Calcutta, and all the way to Assam in the east, where my uncle was Bishop of Assam. He liked the idea of me making recordings on the way, and so was born the radio programme which I would broadcast, called *A Journey to Assam*.

The producer arranged for me to spend a day with a BBC engineer learning how to operate a tape-recorder. They then sent me away with this exceedingly heavy EMI tape-recorder slung onto my back and a bag of nine hours' worth of tapes.

On the eve of our departure I made my first fruitless attempt at getting my piano diploma. After it was over, I came out into the bright sunshine of the outside world and, for many moments, completely lost my memory. I didn't know how to find my way to the Tube station – a straight route I had been taking since I was thirteen years old. I stood and stood and stood – and finally asked the way.

Chapter 14

Journey to Assam

'As the plane landed in Delhi, I saw a monkey bounding over the airport roof, and I knew I was back in India at last.' That's how my prim, queen-like voice started the programme that was later broadcast.

Although I was returning to the land of my birth, I didn't feel as though I had either come home or gone abroad. I was neither a returning citizen nor a holidaymaker. India and England were merged in my mind in a curious sort of way, as one country; an extension of my personal territory. I never had strong feelings of nationality. People used to ask, 'Do you have to choose who you are, English or Indian?' A popular Anglo-Indian novelist between the Thirties and Sixties was John Masters. One of his books, *Bhowani Junction*, which was about the love between a British man and an Anglo-Indian woman, dealt with this dilemma. But I never felt as though it applied to me. There was no cultural gap to leap; no choice to make. I didn't have to change the way I thought, dress or behave when I was in England or in India. Because India was so inclusive of all kinds of sects, races and religions, there was no particular code of dress – except one of basic decency and respect. So for me, India and England were as much merged into one country as my Indian and English blood.

'I saw a monkey bounding over the airport roof,' I was to report. Suddenly, in that one image seen through the aeroplane window, I glimpsed the essence of what India means to me; the way animals and humans live their lives interwoven with each other. In my fantasies I was like Kipling's Mowgli in *The Jungle Book*, living with wolves, leopards, tigers and monkeys; running and hunting, swinging through the jungle canopy, crawling along branches, leaping over rocks. Somehow I sensed that somewhere in the unreachable, incommunicable soul of the wild animal, which stares out at you through its beautiful, translucent, dispassionate eyes, there is a connection with the very beginnings of creation. I felt that so long as we still live among animals, and they live among us, we retain a link with our own origins and, if there is a Creator, to the Creator itself. This intense desire to communicate with wild animals seems very deep in us. Mowgli communicates, because Kipling sought the commonality between animals and humans; that all living species protect their young. Perhaps Kipling felt the same curiosity and helplessness as I did about never really knowing what goes on inside the mind of a wild animal – or indeed other human beings, who often seemed as alien as wild animals.

If I was unable to experience any kind of religious faith as an adolescent growing up in England, in India it's a part of the whole fabric of existence. Every time I go there, I am much more aware of an invisible curtain which, if I drew it aside, maybe I would discover faith – or perhaps not. Wherever I've been, in England or in India, my near-religious experiences have found me, not me them. And I still hesitate over the word 'religious' as it implies an acceptance of a faith in something specific, a doctrine which has been laid down; whereas I think what I experience through a piece of music, looking at an English wheat field rippling in the wind, staring into the eyes of a wild animal, watching an Indian dancer almost incarnating into a god, is a kind of ecstasy which is of the unfathomable, unproven soul.

So I opened up my tape-recorder and plugged in the microphone and began to record, knowing deep inside that I was trying to capture something intangible – and which maybe didn't even exist, except in my head – and yet what the microphone picked up was existence itself. Street sounds: market sellers shouting their wares; the *jingle jangle* of bells around a horse's neck as, like a tap dancer, it clattered down the road, the delicate sound of its hooves revealing its small, bony size; the sound of the motorcycle rickshaws, with their croaky horns; a lone flautist playing his wooden Indian flute in a park; the man at dawn, washing himself at a roadside tap, singing as he splashed the chill water over his gaunt, glistening body – all these conjured up images almost more powerful than any photograph.

Our five weeks in India was dominated by the train. To cover ground and see all our relatives we had to live, eat and sleep on the train. My tape-recorder hoarded hundreds of different sounds; the frantic shriek of the train siren as it came in and out of stations, the platforms seething into life with hawkers and food sellers and chai wallahs (tea sellers) and pleading beggars. As the journey unfolded, moving from place to place, often into the countryside, I recorded singers, dancers, priests at prayer; the mutterings of supplicants making their ablutions in the holy River Ganges, the splash of oars from the boatman as he rowed us among scattered flowers, floating with the ash of the newly cremated from the funeral pyres along the river banks.

It was like listening to a musical score: the distant hoot of the flour mill grinding the wheat; the monkey man and his rattle drum; the splashing buckets hitting the sides of the well as the women drew their water; the washermen at the river, chanting their song as they pounded the clothes against the rocks. In nine hours of tape I had barking dogs, cawing crows, shrieking parrots, the desperate clamour of an Indian dawn which, to me, always seem to encapsulate the desperate wail a baby gives after birth – the wail of sentient beings knowing that, from now on, life will be a struggle to be heard, to be seen, to be fed and to survive.

On that journey to Assam, India unwound herself like an endless glittering sari from the Taj Mahal, to Delhi, to Calcutta, and across the great Brahmaputra River by ferry to the state of Assam, then back via Darjeeling and Kalimpong, dominated by that heart-stopping snow-enveloped mountain, Kanchenjunga, looming out of the Himalayan range. The memory of those mountains, the people, and the drive back down – seeing horsemen and traders on the way, wearing fur-lined Tibetan caps and embroidered jackets, herding their tinkling goats and trains of clattering mules – is as embedded in my memory as a diamond in its setting.

And yet, even as I recorded all these sounds, I felt that frustration of separation. I could no more enter into the essence of India than I could connect with the gaze of a wild animal. I would always be an outsider. It made me realise how English I was inside, though I never felt I had the right to say, 'I am English'. I never said 'we' meaning 'we, the English', or 'us'. Nor did I ever use those words in India. Sometimes I yearned to say 'my – mine'.

The Anglo-Indian novelist John Masters talked of 'choice' – but I had no choice. I didn't choose my parents; I didn't choose the culture which was imbued in me from the cradle by my mother. I didn't choose my language or the colour of my skin. If my cultural allegiance is to the English language, it's because it was the tongue of my mother and my mother tongue; it was my father's language in the household and it was his belief that, though he was an equally superb Urdu-speaker, it was important that we speak English – so I didn't even have a fluent Indian language. Without an Indian language, how could I ever feel Indian?

Perhaps to feel Indian, I should have been a dancer of the classical dance, Bharata Natyam. I would have tried to be the best – that is to say, I would have tried to reach that level of technical perfection, and mastered the language of the gods, so that when I danced, I would be in total communication with them. Only then would I have achieved the highest state of ecstasy and bliss: only then might I have achieved 'faith', for to dance Indian classical dance is to believe in the gods; to incarnate and become one of them; to have faith.

Later, when I was working for the BBC, I was helping to make a film about Shanta Rao, at that time one of India's greatest dancers of Bharata Natyam. I had been waiting in the wings for her to emerge from her dressing room, where she had been locked away all afternoon in prayer and meditation. I knocked gently on her door to tell her it was time. We waited, looked at each other anxiously; there was silence. Then suddenly the door opened, and this supreme woman seemed to glide out of her dressing room and onto the stage. I swear her feet never touched the ground. At that moment, Shanta Rao was no longer a mere human, but had transformed into the goddess she was now dancing.

I went to English-speaking schools, read English books about English characters. England was the heart of the Empire; the heart of the English-speaking world. It was its home. Many immigrants coming into Britain from the colonies thought they were coming 'home'. In truth, I was English in every respect, except for my Indian though Anglophile father, and the colour of my skin.

And perhaps, further proof that I may be suffering from the nostalgia of the outsider, I see the India I love disappearing, as the pace of industrialization rampages ahead like a juggernaut. My India, my past, is becoming the stuff of myth and legend, of romance and fantasy. The wild animals have almost gone; their habitat has almost gone. Mowgli's jungle is now almost non-existent. How glad I was to see places like the vast stretches of the Brahmaputra River before it was bridged; the Taj Mahal, before it had become commercialised; that I could carry away images which were strong enough to outlast the changes which were taking place so rapidly.

Chapter 15

Facing the Music

I have a deep affection for Trinity College of Music, Mandeville Place, London – as it was then. The nearest Tube was Bond Street on the Central Line, on which I could sit and dream all the way to and from Ealing Broadway. Bond Street Tube station exits on to Oxford Street, and each day I passed the shops, noted the fashions, longed for the day when I would have enough money to indulge myself. Trinity College saw me grow up from a schoolgirl into a young woman. It was the witness and the overseer of my musical and mental development. It brought me wonderful friendships.

Despite my struggles with piano, I was fully engaged with what was going on in the musical world – particularly helped by my composer friends, who were right up to date with who was doing what and where. New composers came into my life: Britten, Schoenberg, Webern, Berg, Mahler, Bartok and Stravinsky.

And Trinity was a very multicultural institution, with students from all over the Commonwealth. Along with my special English friends like Jim, a gifted composer, and Jane, a fine musician who shared my mad sense of humour, there was Marina from Hong Kong and Margerida from Goa. Perhaps this is why I was unaware of any overt racism, though I have a memory which still engenders guilt in me from that time.

Waiting for the Tube on an Underground station late one night, a black man approached me to make conversation. I was brusque, and leaped onto the train as soon as the doors opened. I saw the desolation in his face and heard his words plaintively asking, 'Why you brown girls always so uppity?'

Why did I feel guilty? Somehow I felt he would have been experiencing all the loneliness of a hostile world – a world of cruel racial prejudice. I had rejected him too, and he read it as my being colour prejudiced.

We music students were all greedy for the latest musical experiences; we turned pages for singers and instrumentalists at the Wigmore Hall, we queued at the Albert Hall to get into the Prom-enade concerts, we queued at the Royal Festival Hall to see the great musicians of their day: pianist Artur Rubinstein playing three concertos in one evening at the Royal Festival Hall! What bravado! Igor Stravinsky conducting his own music (it was as exciting as if we were going to see Beethoven), Henry Wood conducting Delius, or Otto Klemperer conducting Beethoven. Music on television was yet to happen, and the only way to see our musical idols was to go to the concerts.

We students had passionate debates among ourselves about serial composition – the so-called Twelve Tone Technique as devised by Arnold

Schoenberg in the 1900s, and his Second Viennese School, which was now part of the experimental avant-garde movement.

Yet if Schoenberg was impossible to understand, it was amazing that, for some people, even Stravinsky was too modern and raucous. After all, the radically modern and controversial ballet music *The Rite of Spring* had been composed as early as 1911. It was a work of genius, but we were still arguing about its merits. Stravinsky took his place in my pantheon of musical gods. I became as passionate about his works as I had of Brahms, and I never forget seeing him – this diminutive, taut, unshowy man, conducting his music-drama *Persephone* at the Royal Festival Hall. As for Schoenberg, we had a sense that there was not even one professor in the whole college prepared to support his system of composing, or even discuss it; and I recall that in our History of Music course we covered the twentieth century in just one class. But for composers, trying to find their voice, it was a crucial time as they listened to the philosophical debates, the battles, the outrage about music 'without tunes', music which was cacophonous and empty – the insults were legion.

But there was no one I knew as widely eclectic and broad-minded as Gladys Puttick. It was she who could play any of the Bach *Forty-Eight Preludes and Fugues* by memory; she who enthused about Ravel and Debussy; she who was a devotee of Wagner, going annually to Germany, to his opera house in Bayreuth in Bavaria; she who got me playing Bartok.

When I got back from India, I asked to be moved from my concert-performing piano teacher over to 'GP' as she was affectionately known. She understood that my confidence was in shreds, and set about building it up again. The best way was to play music which was relatively unknown, but which was brilliant and flashy; which would impress an audience, yet without it being too testing to play, bringing instant gratification to both performer and listener. It worked. Composers like Alexander Tcherepnin started me off, followed rapidly by Bartok, Ravel and Debussy, all of whom became part of my repertoire, which I was performing regularly at the weekly college concerts.

Once again, I began to prepare for the elusive Licentiate diploma – and this time I was successful. I can remember the works I played: Bach's *Prelude and Fugue in A minor Bk 1*, César Franck's *Prelude, Chorale and Fugue*, and Lennox Berkeley's *Concert Study in E Flat*. I played the full repertoire by heart – and I knew I'd played well. I could feel it in my bones. I'd felt in control of the keyboard. I had been immersed in the music, and my technique was fully adequate. At the end, just before I left the room, the examiner commented, 'You seem to have a great affinity with western music.'

Every now and then throughout my life, it is such a comment that makes me realise that the way other people see me is not the way I see myself. The examiner was seeing me as someone foreign and from an alien background who nonetheless seemed able to perform western music with an 'affinity'.

I have no idea to this day how much this perception of me has either helped or hindered me. I have never wanted to dwell on the possibility of slights or even outright prejudice; never wanted to seem like an apologist or a victim. But could it be that once, when I entered a piano competition I was discriminated against?

It was only a local county competition and, in my opinion, I'd played infinitely better than anyone else there, and had also known the music more thoroughly than any of the others. I was the only one to play by heart. I gave a performance, whereas the others gave a reading. I was so sure I'd won.

It is important to build up in yourself an ability to view your performance objectively; to be self-critical. Usually you know when you've done well, or not as well, or badly. You don't need the finishing line to tell you you've come first, or someone wagging a finger to tell you you've done wrong, but you have to be able to take criticism; to be judged by a third party. I believe this is the most important reason for taking exams and entering competitions. It's not just the passing or the failing, but the learning to take criticism and to be self-critical. If you're honest inside, you know it.

Just as I knew I had performed well in my diploma, so I knew I'd played well for this competition. Yet when the results were given out I was not even among the first four; I was not even commended.

I was shocked to the point of paranoia. Had I so misjudged myself? I wanted to confront the adjudicator and ask him where I had fallen short. Perhaps if there had been some sort of critique I could have accepted the result; but this was a case of where 'the adjudicator's decision is final'. It haunted me for years because I had no reasons – even false reasons – for the decision.

So, along with the euphoria of success, I knew the taste of failure – rejection even. Not just failure at school, but failure in the one area I thought I couldn't fail in. Oddly, never once, not once, did it shake my belief that music must always be in my life. As for being a performer, I was neutral about it. I had no illusions as to what it would take. I had no illusions that I was anywhere near being ready, or indeed had the right personality. It had never been my ambition, but I had an appetite for taking on the challenge and running with it as far as I could go, simply because I loved nothing more than playing the piano.

So, I shrugged off my setbacks and, having at last got my diploma, I triumphantly set about trying for a French Government Scholarship to study with Jacques Février in Paris.

Chapter 16

Goals

So long as I had goals, I was able to direct my energies and do everything I could to achieve them. But I was still shaky. I could no longer march onto a platform and play with that confidence that I had when I was sixteen. Through my years at college I had become so nervous that before every public performance, no matter how modest, I turned into a quivering jelly. I tried to argue to myself that this was par for the course. As a student, I had turned pages and seen many public performers, and had often noticed very severe nerves.

I once attended a Wigmore Hall recital where

the pianist was playing (my) Brahms *Rhapsody Op. 79*. She came to the repeat at the end of the first section, went back to the start, but on reaching the same point, needed the second time bar to change key and carry on. She just could not get into that second time bar and went back to the beginning twice more, before giving up, having to leave the platform to get her music.

Even my gods were not immune. I once turned pages for Benjamin Britten, when he was performing Schubert with his partner, the tenor Peter Pears. Where beforehand, Pears was calm and self-contained, Britten was nervously downing whisky in the green room. I followed them out onto the platform and took my place to the side of the piano. To my horror, Britten's hands were shaking as he arranged his music on the stand. The piano began the opening section. His hands shook all the way down. I was braced for a disaster, but at the point of his fingers touching the keys, they became entirely firm and under control, and he played with faultless beauty.

Now, here I was, needing all my control to play

well enough to be awarded a scholarship to study with Jacques Février.

Why Jacques Février? I had attended a recital during my year in Lausanne given by a young English pianist called Valeric Tryon. I went round afterwards to get her autograph, and told her that I too wanted to study piano.

'Go to Jacques Février in Paris,' she advised; in her opinion, the best teacher around. It became my goal.

I presented myself before the adjudicators in a small concert room at the French Consulate. I played Debussy's *Images*, and then told them I wanted to study with Jacques Février – not because, I said rather boldly, of learning how to play French music. I told them that I didn't know anyone who played Debussy better than the German, Walter Gieseking. But because I'd been told that Février was the very best teacher.

Perhaps it was because I thought I hadn't any chance of succeeding that I was relaxed, almost fatalistic.

A few weeks later, I heard they had awarded me a scholarship.

My teenage years had ended. I was setting off for Paris. I was almost free; almost independent. In a strange way, I was prepared for the bumpy road ahead; for a life full of failures and disasters, of huge setbacks and important triumphs. Throughout it all, my life would be lived with music; I held on to music when I went to work at the BBC and, even later, when I became a writer – somehow, I always had to feel a musical impulse somewhere in my story. Music would always be at the heart of my goals; dictate my journey, and be the greatest source of inspiration.

I will never say that I loved music for the comfort or solace it gave me; not as something to cheer me up, or as a simple skill whether for pleasure or as a professional. It was far, far more than that. It was never there to serve me, but for me to serve it. Just as a mountain is not there for my benefit, but to challenge me; to beckon me to its peaks, and to show me panoramas I never knew existed. Perhaps it is the only thing in which I had complete faith.

Towards the end of her life, my mother used to ask me, 'Did I make a mistake? Should we have stayed in India?' Each time she asked, I rethought my answer, but in the end, I always said, 'No, you were right to leave.' I was a daydreamer, yes – and I walked on my hands. And when I walked on my two feet, I didn't just walk, I strode; I sometimes ran – not the ways, in those times, of an Indian woman.

India and England may have been one territory in my mind, but I was very clear then in which bit I wanted to live. I lived and thought western. I knew I could never have lived as an Indian woman.

Daydreamer, and topsy-turvy that I am, I'm glad we came to England, because I would rather be not quite English in England, than not quite Indian in India. I have been able to explore my Indian roots far more easily by visiting India than I feel would have been possible the other way round. I have been able to discover India and squirrel away my passions for so much of it. India will never feel an alien land to me. It is literally in my blood. I love its mountains and valleys, its plains and villages, its incredible energy and exuberance, its temples and paintings, and – especially – its music and dance. How can I ever express how moved and entranced I am by India. But here in England, I'm learning to say, 'me', 'my', 'ours', 'mine'. I've been here over fifty years – time enough to claim ownership, enough to belong.

I think about the concept of time. For me, life and time are more than a river flowing by in one direction: life to death. There are so many ways of living in time. I am so often upside down and back to front; rushing forward, and then having to retrace my steps to fill in things I have missed out on the way, discovering new things, reassessing my past. As the German author Goethe said, 'Life can only be understood backwards, but it must be lived forwards.' Even, I would add, if it is lived upside down, walking on your hands.

OUT OF INDIA

Jamila Gavin

Vivid memories of an Anglo-Indian childhood, by the award-winning author of Coram Boy.

I am truly a child of both countries and both cultures.

Born to an Indian father and an English mother, Jamila Gavin's childhood was divided between two worlds.

Her earliest memories are of India, where she lived in a crumbling palace built for a prince, and learned to steal sugar cane and suck mangoes. But she would spend much of her childhood in England, where she picked blackberries, got chilblains, and learned to recognise doodlebug bombs. And between the two there were unforgettable journeys, by bullock carts and tongas, crowded trains and romantic P&O liners.

A touching and very personal recollection, with a backdrop of world-shaking events, from the Blitz of World War II to the struggle for Indian independence and the assassination of Gandhi.

Illustrated with the author's own delightful photographs.